DIRECTORY
OF STATE AND LOCAL
HISTORY
PERIODICALS

OFFICIALLY
DISCARDED

Compiled by

Milton Crouch

and

Hans Raum

R
973
cop.1

Chicago

American Library Association

1977

Library of Congress Cataloging in Publication Data

Crouch, Milton, 1937-
    Directory of state and local history periodicals.

    Includes index.
    1. United States--History, Local--Periodicals--
Directories. I. Raum, Hans, 1940-   joint author.
II. Title.
Z1250.C76   [E180]   973'.05   77-4396
ISBN 0-8389-0246-4

Printed in the United States of America

TABLE OF CONTENTS

INTRODUCTION

This directory lists state and local history periodicals currently being published in the United States and provides information on published and unpublished indexes to these periodicals. Also included are major local historical periodicals which are no longer being published but which were indexed in national indexes during their existence.

Most of the titles contained in this directory are not listed in Ulrich's International Periodicals Directory. Titles for which we have less than complete information are listed because of the value in making their existence known and identifying them by state.

The user should be aware that an article appearing in a local history journal may not be included in a national index or abstracting service for as long as two to three years after

the publication of the article. Several of the
indexes to history periodicals cited in this
directory select only those articles appearing
on specific topics. Indexes such as <u>Abstracts</u>
<u>of Folklore Studies</u>, <u>Women Studies Abstracts</u>,
<u>Abstracts of English Studies</u> are all highly se-
lective. For this reason we have included,
when possible, the dates of actual coverage by
the index cited.

    National indexes include only a minority
of the local history journals being published.
<u>Writings on American History</u> was not published
for 1904-05, 1941-47, 1962-72. Fortunately,
Krause-Thomson Organization has recently published the volumes covering 1962 through 1972.
<u>America: History and Life</u>, published by the
American Bibliographical Center, Santa Barbara,
California is a distinct improvement over pre-
vious indexes to historical literature because
it is an abstracting service. However, some
local history titles are only given an annual
scope note instead of being selectively or com-
pletely indexed.

The following method was used to compile
the information contained in this directory. A
preliminary listing of local historical society
publications was obtained from the ninth and
tenth editions of the Directory of Historical
Societies and Agencies in the United States.
Preliminary indexing information was obtained
at this point by checking the periodical titles
indexed in Writings on American History, Historical Abstracts, America: History and Life,
the H. W. Wilson indexes and other relevant
guides such as the Michigan Magazine Index,
New Jersey Periodical Index, etc.

A letter was sent to every state historical society asking them for a listing of the
local historical societies within the state
publishing a journal. The state agencies were
able to supply us with some information regard-
ing the indexing of local history journals.
After obtaining information from fifty state
historical societies we compiled a listing of
all the local historical societies in the United States having a journal or newsletter. A

questionnaire was sent to each local historical society publishing a journal or newsletter. This questionnaire enabled the compilers to ascertain the beginning date of the publication, the correct title, the frequency, and indexing information. A copy of the publication was requested. At this point all titles gleaned so far were checked in the <u>Union List of Serials</u>, <u>New Serial Titles</u>, <u>National Union Catalog</u> and Ulrich's to establish entry and title changes.

The guide took final shape after listing all local historical society publications by state. Each entry listing was sent to the state historical society or the state library for an evaluation and any additional information they might have.

We hope that this directory will help make the body of historical periodicals more accessible to anyone interested in American local history.

ACKNOWLEDGEMENTS

The support given to us by the Executive Board of the Reference and Adult Services Division of the American Library Association is deeply appreciated. We wish to extend special thanks to Dr. John Bodger, Chairman of the Bibliography and Indexes Committee of the History Section; Mildred V. Schulz, Librarian, Illinois State Historical Library; Lucile Boykin, Dallas Public Library; and Marianne L. Feldman, Oregon Historical Society. Lee Ash, always one to offer encouragement and good advice, inspired us to begin and to complete

LIST OF ABBREVIATIONS

A	Annual
Assoc.	Association
Ave.	Avenue
B-E	Biennial
B-M	Bimonthly
Bldg.	Building
Co.	County
Comm.	Commission
Ct.	Court
Dept.	Department
Div.	Division
Dr.	Drive
Found.	Foundation
Ft.	Fort
Hist.	Historical
Hwy.	Highway
Inst.	Institute
Irreg.	Irregular
M	Monthly
Mus.	Museum
n. s.	new series
Q	Quarterly
Rd.	Road
Rm.	Room
Rt.	Route
S-A	Semi-annual
Soc.	Society
St.	Street, Saint
Univ.	University
v.	volume (s)

ALABAMA

The Alabama Baptist Historian
                              1964-   S-A $1
     Samford Univ., Birmingham, 35209. Ed.
F. W. Helmbold. Contemplate the preparation
of a 10-yr. index.

The Alabama Historical Quarterly
                              1930-   Q
     Alabama State Dept. of Archives and
Hist., 624 Washington Ave., Montgomery,
36104. Publication suspended 1931-39. Cumulative index, 1930-44, 1945-58; index at
end of each volume. Indexed in Abstracts
of English Studies, 1971-; Writings on American History, 1939, 1951-; America: History
and Life, 1963-; Abstracts of Folklore
Studies, 1967, 1970-.

The Alabama Review
                              1948-   Q $5
     Auburn Univ., Hist. Dept., Auburn,
36830. Cumulative index, 1948-57. A second
index is under consideration. Indexed in
Writings on American History, 1948-; America:
History and Life, 1963-; Abstracts of English
Studies, 1963-69, 1972-; Abstracts of Folklore Studies, 1964, 1966, 1969, 1971-.

A Journal of History
                              1972-   Q $7.50
     West Jefferson Co. Hist. Soc., 1830 4th
Ave. S., Bessemer, 35020. Annual index.
Cumulative index on cards.

Journal of Muscle Shoals History
                    1973-   A $2.50
        Tennessee Valley Hist. Soc., Sheffield,
    35660.   Index in each issue.

Papers of the Pike County Historical Society
                    1955-   A $4
        Pike Co. Hist. Soc., 200 Richmond Ave.,
    Troy, 36081.   Ed. Margaret P. Farmer.

Trails in History
                    1969-   Q $10
        Lee Co. Hist. Soc., Alabama State Rd.
    14, Loachapoka, 36865.   Ed. Alexander Nunn.

                    ALASKA

Alaska History News
                    1970-   B-M
        Not indexed.

Alaska Journal
                    1971-   Q $8
        Alaska North West Pub. Co., Box 4EEE,
    Anchorage, 99509.   Annual index compiled
    but not published.   Plans are to publish a
    quinquennial cumulative index.   Indexed in
    Northern Titles-KWIC Index, 1973- (Boreal
    Inst. for Northern Studies, Univ. of Al-
    berta, Edmonston, Canada); Abstracts of
    Folklore Studies, 1972-.

The Discoverer
        Cordova Hist. Soc., 1st and A Sts.,
    Cordova, 99574.

Tongass Historical Society Newsletter
                    1961-   Q $5
        Box 674, Ketchikan, 99901.   Ed. Pat
    Roppel.   Not indexed.

University of Alaska Museum Newsletter
                    1964-75 Irreg.
        Fairbanks, 99701.

ARIZONA

Arizona and the West
                    1959-   Q $5
        Univ. of Arizona, The Library, Rm. 310,
    Tucson, 85721. Cumulative index, 1959-63.
    Indexed in Writings on American History,
    1960, 1973-; America: History and Life,
    1963-; Women Studies Abstracts, 1972-.

Arizona Historical Review
                    1928-36 Q
        Indexed in Writings on American History,
    1930-36.

Bucksin Bulletin
                    1958-   Q $5
        Westerners International, Univ. Station,
    Box 3941, Tucson, 85717. Not indexed.

Cochise Quarterly
                    1971-   Irreg.
        Cochise Co. Hist. and Archaeological
    Soc., Box 818, Douglas, 85607. Not indexed.

Graham County Historical Society Journal
                    1965-   A
        808 8th Ave., Safford, 85546.

Journal of Arizona History
                    1960-   Q $7.50
        Formerly Arizoniana, 1960-64. Arizona
    Hist. Soc., 949 E. 2nd St., Tucson, 85719.
    Annual index, v. 6-. Cumulative index, v.
    1-5. Indexed in America: History and Life,
    1963-.

Newsletter of the Casa Grande Valley Historical Society   1970-   Irreg. $7.50
        404 N. Marshall St., Casa Grande, 85222.
Ed. Glenn Tiller. Not indexed.

Plateau
                        1928-   Q $7.50
        Northern Arizona Soc. of Science and
Art, Rt. 4, Box 720, Flagstaff, 86001. Ed.
Richard Ach. Quadrennial indexes. Indexed
in Abstracts in Anthropology; Writings on
American History, 1939-.

Smoke Signal
                        1956-   M $2.50
        Colorado River Indian Tribes Mus. Li-
brary, Rt. 1, Box 23-B, Parker, 85344. Ed.
Daphene G. Peck. Not indexed.

Wagon Train Report
        Pioneer Arizona, Phoenix, 85061.

                    ARKANSAS

Arkansas Historical Quarterly
                        1942-   Q $6
        Arkansas Hist. Assoc., Univ. of Ar-
kansas, Dept. of Hist., Fayetteville, 72701.
Ed. Walter L. Brown. Annual index, 1962-.
Cumulative index, v. 1-15. Master index on
cards. Indexed in Writings on American
History, 1948-60, 1973-; America: History
and Life, 1964-.

Arkansas Valley Historical Quarterly
                        1954-   Q

Benton County Historical Society Pioneer
                        1954-   Q $4
        109 N. Madison, Siloam Springs, 72761.
Ed. Mrs. Melvin Smith. Cumulative index.

Butterfield Overland Mail Bag
    Butterfield Trail Memorial Assoc., Box
108, Eureka Springs, 72632.

Carroll County Historical Quarterly
                    1955-   Q $5
    304 Rose Rd., Berryville, 72616.   Ed.
O. K. Braswell.   Cumulative index.

Civil War Round Table Digest
                    1968-   M $7.50
    Civil War Round Table Assoc., Box 7388,
Little Rock, 72207.   Ed. J. L. Russell.   Not
indexed.

Clark County Historical Journal
                    1973-   Q

Craighead County Historical Quarterly
                    1962-   Q $5
    Box 1011, Jonesboro, 72401.   Ed. Mrs.
Phyllis Morse.   Cumulative index in manu-
script form.

Faulkner Facts and Fiddlings
                    1959-   Q
    Faulkner Co. Hist. Soc., Conway, 72032.
Cumulative index, v. 1-5.

Flashback
                                      $5
    Washington Co. Hist. Soc., Box 357,
Fayetteville, 72701.   Ed. Mrs. Jean Newhouse.

Grand Prairie Historical Society Bulletin
                    S-A

Greene County Historical Quarterly
                    1964-   Q

The Heritage
                    1957-   Q
    Crawford Co. Hist. Soc., 1012 Cedar St.,
Van Buren, 72956.   Cumulative index on cards.

Heritage of Stone
                              1972-   Q $3
     Stone Co. Hist. Soc., Mountain View,
72560.

Independence County Chronicle
                              1960-   Q $4
     Independence Co. Hist. Soc., Box 1412,
Batesville, 72501. Ed. A. C. McGinnis.

Izard County Historian
                              1970-   Q $4
     Izard Co. Hist. Soc., Dolph, 72528.
Ed. Mrs. Helen C. Lindley. Cumulative index
on cards.

Jefferson County Historical Quarterly
                                       Q
     Formerly Jefferson County Historical
Magazine. Indexed in Writings on American
History, 1940, 1950-57, 1960.

Ouachita County Historical Quarterly
                              1958-   Q

Phillips County Historical Quarterly
                                       Q $5
     623 Pecan St., elena, 72342.

Pulaski County Historical Review
                              1953-   Q
     653 Palm St., Little Rock, 72202.
Indexes for early issues on cards.

Record
                              1960-   A $5
     Garland Co. Hist. Soc., 914 Summer St.,
Hot Springs, 71901. Annual index.

Reflections
                              1969-   B-M
     Arkansas Hist. Comm., 300 W. Markham
St., 72201. Not indexed.

Stream of History
>> 1963- Q $3
>> Jackson Co. Hist. Soc., 314 Vine St.,
Newport, 72112.

White County Heritage
>> 1962- Q
>> Annual index, v. 1-3.

CALIFORNIA

Adobe Trails
>> 1965- Q $7
>> Hayward Area Hist. Soc., Box 555, Hayward, 94541. Not indexed.

Bridge
>> La Puente Valley Hist. Soc.

Las Calaveras
>> 1952- Q $5
>> Calaveras Co. Hist. Soc., 16 Main St., San Andres, 95249. Ed. Willard P. Fuller, Jr. Not indexed.

California Historian
>> 1954-
>> Formerly Conference of California Historical Societies Newsletter. Conference of California Hist. Societies. Indexed in America: History and Life, 1964-; Abstracts of Folklore Studies, 1970-.

California Historical Courier
>> 1973- 7/yr. $7
>> Formerly California Historical Society Notes. California Hist. Soc., 2090 Jackson St., San Francisco, 94109. Not indexed.

California Historical Quarterly
                         1922-   Q $17.50
     California Hist. Soc.,2090 Jackson
St., San Francisco, 94109. Ed. Marilyn
Ziebarth. Annual index. Cumulative index
1922-1961. Indexed in Writings on American
History, 1922-; Historical Abstracts, 1954-;
1963; America: History and Life, 1964-;
Abstracts of Folklore Studies, 1972,1974-.

La Campana
                         1964-   Q
     Santa Barbara Trust for Historic
Preservation, 2635 Homestead Rd., Santa
Clara, 95051. Annual index.

Chinese Historical Society of America Bulletin
                         1966-   10/yr
     17 Adler Place, San Francisco, 94133.

Chispa
                         1961-   Q $5
     Formerly Tuolumne County Historical
Society Quarterly. Box 695, Sonora, 95370.
Ed. C. M. Deferrari. Not indexed.

Covered Wagon
                         1943-   Q $10
     Shasta Hist. Soc., Redding, 96001.
   Ed. Jean Beauchamp. Not indexed.

Cross and Cockade Journal
                         1960-   Q $9
     Cross and Cockade Soc. of World War
One Aero Historians, 10443 S. Memphis Ave.,
Whittier, 90604. Ed. George H. Cooke.
Indexed in Writings on American History,
1960.

Diggins
                         1957-   Q $8
     Butte Co. Hist. Soc., Courthouse,
Oroville, 95965. Ed. Virginia Parker. Cumulative indexes v.1-8, 1957-64; v.9-13, 1965-
69.

Fairview Register
                        1972-   M
        Costa Mesa Hist. Soc., Costa Mesa, 92627.
    Ed. Mildred Mathews. Not indexed.

Los Fierros
                        1966-   Irreg.
        La Casa De Rancho Los Cerritos, 6400
    Bixby Hill Rd., Long Beach, 90807. Not in-
    dexed.

Forest History
                        1957-   Q $10
        Forest Hist. Soc., Santa Cruz, 95061.
    Ed. Douglas Davis. Cumulative author index
    in July 1973 issue. Indexed in Writings on
    American History, 1960-; America: History and
    life, 1967-.

Gleanings
                        1966-   Irreg. $5
        Formerly Napa County Historical Society
    Notes. 928 Coombs St., Napa, 94558. Ed.
    Frederick Pond. Not indexed.

Historic Kern
                        1948-   Q
        Kern Co. Hist. Soc., Box 141, Bakers-
    field, 93301. Ed. Norman Berg.

Journal of San Diego History
                        1955-   Q $10
        Formerly Quarterly, v. 1-10/1955-64;
    Times Gone By, v. 11, 1965. San Diego Hist.
    Soc., Box 81825, San Diego, 92138. Ed. J. E.
    Moss. Annual index. Cumulative index on
    cards. Indexed in Writings on American
    History, 1960, 1973-.

Journal of the American Aviation Historical
Society   1956-   Q $12.50
        Box 456, Chatsworth, 91311. Annual in-
    dex. Cumulative index, v. 1-10. Indexed in
    Air University Library Index to Military Per-
    iodicals.

Landmark
                          1961-   Q
     El Monte Hist. Soc., 3100 N. Tyler Ave.,
El Monte, 91731. Annual index.

Madera County Historian
                          1961-   Irreg. $3
210 W. Yosemite Ave., Madera, 93637. Ed.
M. Lindemann. Occasional indexes.

Mains'l Haul
                          Q $12
     Maritime Mus. Assoc. of San Diego, 1306
N. Harbor Dr., San Diego, 92101. Ed. Jerry
MacMullen. Not indexed.

Mendocino County Historical Society Newsletter
                          1961-   B-M $3
     243 Bush St., Fort Bragg, 95437. Ed.
T. O. Moungovan. Cumulative index.

News and Notes
                          1954-   3/yr. $5
     Santa Cruz Hist. Soc., Box 246, Santa
Cruz, 95061. Ed. Bruce Meacham. Cumulative
index in preparation.

Noticias
                          1958-   Q $10
     Santa Barbara Hist. Soc., 136 E. De la
Guerra St., Santa Barbara, 93101. Ed.
Robert Gates. Cumulative index on cards.
Indexed in America: History and Life, 1965-.

Old Gables and Tarnished Doorknobs
                          1971-   Q
     Redwood City Heritage Assoc., 627
Hamilton St., Redwood City, 94064.

Pacific Coast Chapter News
                          1937-   M
     Pacific Coast Railway and Locomotive
Hist. Soc. Not indexed.

Pacific Historian
                              1957-   Q $6
        Univ. of the Pacific, Stockton, 95204.
Ed. Martha Seffer O'Bryon. Indexed in Ab-
stracts of Folklore Studies, 1971-; America:
History and Life, 1964-.

Pacific Historical Review
                              1932-   Q $8
        Pacific Coast Branch, American Histor-
ical Association, University of California
Press, 2223 Fulton St., Berkeley, 94720.
Ed. N. C. Hundley. Annual index. Cumula-
tive index in preparation. Indexed in Social
Sciences and Humanities Index, 1932-; Histor-
ical Abstracts, 1954-63; America: History and
Life, 1964-; Social Science Citation Index;
Writings on American History, 1932-.

Past and Present
                              1958-   Q $6
        Formerly Fresno and Present. Fresno
Co. Hist. Soc., 7160 W. Kearney Blvd.,
Fresno, 93717. Ed. Benjamin Bencomo. Not
indexed.

Pasttimer
        Marin Co. Hist. Soc.

La Peninsula
                              1941-   3/yr.
        San Mateo Co. Hist. Assoc., San Mateo,
94402. Cumulative index in photocopy.

Placer Nugget
        Placer Co. Hist. Soc.

Pomona Valley Historian
        Hist. Soc. of Pomona Valley, Inc.

El Pueblo Gazette
                              Ceased 1972
        El Pueblo de Los Angeles State Hist-
oric Park Comm.

Los Ranchos
                              1948-   Q $2
     Moraga Hist. Soc., Box 103, Moraga,
94556. Not indexed.

Rear View Mirror
                              1965-   Irreg.
     Atascadero Hist. Soc., Box 1047, Ata-
scadero, 93422. Not indexed.

San Joaquin Historian
                              1963-   Q $8
     Formerly Bulletin. San Joaquin Hist.
Soc., 11793 N. Micke Grove Rd., Lodi, 95240.
Ed. R. Bonta. Not indexed.

San Leandro Recollections
                              1969- B-M
     San Leandro Hist. Soc., 471 Superior
Ave., San Leandro, 94577. Ed. Brent Gallo-
way. Cumulative index.

Siskiyou Pioneer
                              1946-   A $4
     Siskiyou Co. Hist. Soc., 910 S. Main
St., Yreka, 96097. Cumulative index, 1946-
71.

Southern California Quarterly
                              1884-   Q
     Hist. Soc. of Southern California, 200
East Ave., Los Angeles, 90031. Ed. D. B.
Nunis. Cumulative index, 1884-1957. Annual
index. Indexed in Writings on American
History, 1915-; Historical Abstracts, 1962-
63; America: History and Life, 1964-.

Spanishtown News
                              1970-   A
     Spanishtown Hist. Soc., Box 62, Half
Moon Bay, 94019.

Tales of the Paradise Ridge
                         1960-   2/yr. $3
     Paradise Fact and Folklore, Inc., 6346
Diamond Ave., Paradise, 95969. Ed. Lois
McDonald.

Tall Tree
                         1949-   Irreg.
     Palo Alto Hist. Assoc., Box 193, Palo
Alto, 94302. Not indexed.

Tidings
                         1971-   M $5
     Napa Co. Hist. Soc., 928 Coombs St.,
Napa, 94558. Ed. Jess Doud. Not indexed.

Traction Gazette
                         1956-   M $3
     Orange Empire Trolley Mus., Box 548,
Perris, 92370. Ed. William Wootton.

Trail
                         1961-   Q
     California Pioneers of Santa Clara Co.,
2221 Coastland Ave., San Jose, 95125.

Tribal Spokesman
                         1969-   M $5
     Inter-Tribal Council of California,
2969 Fulton Ave., Sacramento, 95821. Not
indexed.

Trinity Trails
                         1955-   A $3
     Trinity Co. Hist. Soc., Main St.,
Weaverville, 96093. Ed. Russ Engel.

Valley
                         1951-   M $10
     San Fernando Valley Hist. Soc., Inc.,
10940 Sepulveda Blvd., Mission Hills, 91340.
Ed. Elva Meline. Not indexed.

Ventura County Historical Society Quarterly
                          1956-   Q $10
      77 N. California St.,   Ventura, 93001.
Ed. G. W. Heil. Two cumulative indexes cover
up to 1970. Indexed in Writings on American
History, 1955-60.

La Vista
                          1968-   S-A
     San Luis Obispo Co. Hist. Soc., 696
Monterey St., San Luis Obispo, 93401. Ed.
Loren Nicholson. Not indexed.

Yolo County Historical Society Newsletter
                                            $8
        Box 1447, Woodland, 95695. Ed. Shawn
Grogan. Not indexed.

                    COLORADO

Arvada Historian
      Arvada Hist. Soc., 6047 Flower St.,
Arvada, 80003.

Colorado Magazine
                      1923-   Q
      State Hist. Soc. of Colorado, 200
14th. Ave., Denver, 80203. Cumulative
indexes, 1923-48; 1949-60(?). Indexed in
Writings on American History, 1923-; America:
History and Life, 1964-; Abstracts of Folklore
Studies, 1965, 1970, 1972-.

Historical Flashbacks
      Fremont-Custer Hist. Soc., Inc., 423
Hazel Ave., Canon City, 81212.

Mountain Diggins
                      1973-   A $10
      Lake Co. Civic Center Assoc., Inc.,
Box 962, Leadville, 80461.

San Luis Valley Historian
                    1969-   Q
        Box 982, Alamosa, 81101. Not indexed.

                    CONNECTICUT

Connecticut Antiquarian
                    1949-   S-A
        Antiquarian and Landmarks Soc. of Con-
    necticut, Inc., 394 Main St. Hartford, 06106.
    Ed. Richard N. Ford. Cumulative index, v. 1-
    20.

Connecticut Bicentennial Gazette
                    1971-   Q
        Connecticut Historical Commission, 59 S.
    Prospect St., Hartford, 16106. Not indexed.

Connecticut Historical Society Bulletin
                    1934-   Q $12
        Formerly Connecticut Historical Society.
    Collections. 1 Elizabeth St., Hartford,
    06105. Ed. Phyllis Kihn. Indexed in Writings
    on American History, 1903, 1907, 1909-60,
    1973-; America: History and Life, 1964-; Ab-
    stracts of English Studies, 1971; Abstracts
    of Folklore Studies, 1967, 1972.

Connecticut History Newsletter
                    1967-   S-A
        Assoc. for the Study of Connecticut
    History. Eastern Connecticut State College,
    Willimantic, 06226. Ed. David M. Roth. June
    1973 Newsletter has a cumulative listing of
    all research projects in Conn. history for
    the period 1967-73; June, 1974 has a cumula-
    tive listing for the period 1967-74.

Connecticut Magazine
                    1895-1908
        Formerly Connecticut Quarterly. Indexed
    in Writings on American History, 1902-03,1906.

Connecticut Valley Historical Society Papers and
Proceedings
       Indexed in Writings on American History,
   1902-03, 1907, 1909.

Echo II
       Simsbury Hist. Soc., 800 Hopmeadow St.,
   Simsbury, 06070.

Gristmill
                          1964-   5/yr.
       Trumbull Hist. Soc., Inc., Box 312, Trum-
   bull, 06611. Not indexed.

Groton Banker
                          1971-   3/yr.
       Groton Bank Hist. Assoc., 5 Meridian St.
   Groton, 06340. Not indexed.

Historical Footnotes
                          1963-   Q
       Stonington Hist. Soc., Box 103, Stoning-
   ton, 06378. Cumulative index.

Hourglass
       Willington Hist. Soc., West Willington,
   06279.

Log
                          1948-   Q
       Mystic Seaport, Inc., Greenmanville Ave.
   Rt. 27, Mystic, 06355. Annual index.

New Canaan Historical Society Annual
                                A
       New Canaan Hist. Soc., 13 Oenoke Ridge,
   New Canaan, 06840. Indexed in Writings on
   American History, 1949-60.

New Haven Colony Historical Society Journal
                          1952-   S-A
       114 Whitney Ave., New Haven, 06510.
   Cumulative index, 1952-68.

New London County Historical Society Quarterly
Bulletin   Q
        Not indexed.

News Notes
                        1962-   Q
        Westport Hist. Soc., 99 Myrtle Ave.,
   Westport, 06880. Not indexed.

Newsletter of the Rocky Hill Historical Society
                        1964-   Irreg.
        Not indexed.

Noank Historical Society Newsletter
                        1967-   Q
        Not indexed.

Old Saybrook Historical Society Bulletin
                        1973-   Q $7.50
        Box 4, Old Saybrook, 06475. Not indexed.

Publick Post
                        1938-   3/yr.
        Formerly Retrospect. Hist. Soc. of
   Glastonbury, Box 56, Glastonbury, 06033.
   Cumulative index.

The Rangelight
                              Irreg. $7.50
        Conference of Connecticut River Hist.
   Societies in Connecticut, Inc., c/o P. J.
   Revill, 460 Old Main St., Rocky Hill, 06067.

Spectator
                        1971-   Q
        Noah Webster Found. and Hist. Soc. of
   West Hartford, Inc., 227 S. Main St., West
   Hartford, 06107. Not indexed.

Vernon Historical Society News
        43 Hale St., Vernon, 06066.

Wadsworth Atheneum Bulletin
                        1965-72 3/yr.

Wind Rose
                    1970-   M
      Mystic Seaport, Inc., Mystic Seaport,
   06355. Ed. Gainor R. Akin. Not indexed.

                    DELAWARE

Delaware History
                    1946-   S-A $15
      Hist. Soc. of Delaware, 505 Market St.,
   Wilmington, 19801. Ed. John A. Munroe.
   Indexed and printed upon completion of a vol.
   of four issues. Indexed in America: History
   and Life, 1968-; Writings on American History
   1948-; Abstracts of English Studies, 1971.

Delaware State Magazine
                    1919-20
      Indexed by Wilmington Inst. and New Cas-
   tle Co. Libraries, April, 1919-March, 1920.

Delaware Today
                    1962-   M $5
      The Devon Suite 1A-1B, 2401 Penn. Ave.,
   Wilmington, 19806. Indexing project planned
   by Wilmington Inst.

Footprints of the Past
                                  $25
      Duck Creek Hist. Soc., Smyrna, 19977.

Fort Delaware Notes
                    1951-   M $4
      Ft. Delaware Soc., Box 1251, Wilmington
   19899. Ed. W. Emerson Wilson. Not indexed.

Harness Magazine
                    1872-77
      Indexed by Wilmington Inst., Sept.,
   1872-Jan., 1877.

Milford Historical Society Newsletter
1963-   S-A $5
     Formerly Kent. 501 N. W. Front St., Mil-
ford, 19963. Ed. M. Catherine Downing. Not
indexed.

Views
1933
     Indexed by Wilmington Inst. May 13-Oct.,
7, 1933.

Wilmington
1926-34
     Indexed by Wilmington Inst. May, 1926-
March, 1934.

DISTRICT OF COLUMBIA

Capitol Studies
1972-   S-A $12
     U. S. Capitol Hist. Soc., 200 Maryland
Ave., N. E. 20015. Index being compiled.

FLORIDA

Apalachee
1944-   Irreg. $5
     Tallahassee Hist. Soc., Florida State
Univ., 32306. Not indexed.

Archives and History Newsletter
1970-   M   Free
     Florida Div. of Archives, Hist. and
Records Management. 401 E. Gaines St.,
Tallahassee, 32301. Ed. Gerald A. Butterfield.

Caloosa Quarterly
                    1972-   Q
     Southwest Florida Hist. Soc., Box 1362,
Ft. Myers, 33902. Not indexed.

El Escribano
                    1955-   Q $3
     St. Augustine Hist. Soc., 271 Charlotte
St., St. Augustine, 32084. Ed. Mark E.
Fretwell. Typewritten index.

Florida Historical Quarterly
                    1908-   Q $10
     Florida Hist. Soc., Box 14045, Univ. of
Florida, Gainesville, 32601. Ed. Samuel
Proctor. Indexed in Writings on American
History, 1908-; Historical Abstracts, 1954-
63; America: History and Life, 1964-.

Martello
                    1964-   Irreg.
     Key West Art and Hist. Soc., S. Roose-
velt Blvd., Key West, 33040. Not indexed.

New River News
                    1962-   M $10
     Ft. Lauderdale Hist. Soc., 850 N. E.
12th Ave., Ft. Lauderdale, 33304. Ed. Mar-
jorie D. Patterson. Annual index included
in society's annual report. Cumulative index on cards.

Orange County Historical Quarterly
                    1959-   Q   Free
     27 E. Central St., Orlando, 32801. Ed.
D. A. Cheney. Not indexed.

Pensacola Historical Society Quarterly
                    1965-   Q $5
     405 S. Adams St., Pensacola, 32501. Ed.
D. Paul Parks. Each issue covers a single
topic. Not indexed.

Sea Breeze
                              1964-   M   Free
        St. Petersburg Hist. Soc., 335 2nd Ave.
N. E., St. Petersburg, 33701. Not indexed.

Tequesta
                              1941-   A $10
        Hist. Assoc. of Southern Florida, 3280
S. Miami Ave., Miami, 33129. Contents listing for 1941-70 in society's office.

Update
                              1973-   B-M $10
        Hist. Assoc. of Southern Florida, 3280
S. Miami Ave., Miami, 33129. Ed. Leonard G.
Pardue. Not indexed.

                          GEORGIA

Atlanta Historical Bulletin
                                              $12
        Atlanta Hist. Soc., 3099 Andrews Dr.,
N. W., Atlanta, 30305. Ed. Franklin M. Gar-
rett.

Awareness
        Ocfuskee Hist. Soc., Inc., Box 1051,
La Grange, 30240.

Georgia Archive
                              1972-   S-A $5
        Soc. of Georgia Archivists, Box 261,
Georgia State Univ., Ed. David B. Gracy, II.

Georgia Historical Association Proceedings
                          1917-18
        Indexed in Writings on American History,
    1917.

Georgia Historical Quarterly
                          1917-   Q $10
     Georgia Hist. Soc., 501 Whitaker St.,
Savannah, 31401. Cumulative index, v. 1-15/
1917-31. Indexed in Writings on American
History, 1917-; Historical Abstracts, 1955-
62; America: History and Life, 1963-.

Georgia Historical Society Collections
                          1840-1916
     Indexed in Writings on American History,
1911-16.

Georgia Historical Society Proceedings
     Formerly its Annals, 1876-77, 1915-16.
Indexed in Writings on American History,
1916-17, 1919.

Georgia Salzburger Society News Letter
                                     $2
     9375 Whitfield Ave., Savannah, 31406.
Ed. Charles A. LeBey.

Historic Savannah Quarterly Newsletter
                          1960-   Q $15
     Historic Savannah Found., Inc., 119
Habersham St., Savannah, 31402.

Northwest Georgia Historical and Genealogical
Quarterly   1969-   Q $6
     Box 2484, Rome, 30161. Ed. Mrs. Jewel
J. Dyer. Cumulative index to v. 1-6 print-
ed in v. 7, no. 1, 1975.

Oak Leaves
                          1970-   B-M $5
     Thomasville Landmarks, Inc., Thomas-
ville, 31792. Ed. Norman C. Larson. Not
indexed.

Richmond County History
                          1969-   S-A $5
     Richmond Co. Hist. Soc., c/o Augusta
College Library, 2500 Walton Way, Augusta,
30904. Index to v. 1-5 in preparation.

View Points
                        1967-   Irreg.
    Georgia Baptist Hist. Soc., Mercer Univ.
Library, Macon, 31207. Cumulative Index on
cards at Mercer Univ. Library.

HAWAII

Hawaiian Journal of History
                        1967-   A $10
    Hawaiian Hist. Soc., 560 Kawaiahas St.
Honolulu, 96813. Not indexed.

Lahaina Jottings
                        1961-   Irreg.
    Lahaina Restoration Found., Box 338,
Hahaina, 96761. Not indexed.

IDAHO

Idaho Yesterdays
                        1957-   Q $5
    Idaho Hist. Soc., 610 N. Julia Davis
Dr., Boise, 83706. Index at end of every
four volumes. Indexed in America: History
and Life, 1963-; Writings on American History, 1957-.

Latah County Museum Society Quarterly Bulletin
                        1971-   Q $25
    110 S. Adams St., Moscow, 83848. Ed.
Kenneth B. Platt. Not indexed.

Owyhee Outpost
                        1970-   A $3
    Owyhee Hist. Soc., Murphy, 83650. Not
indexed.

Snake River Echos

                              1976-   Q $5
     Formerly Upper Snake River Valley
Historical Society Quarterly, 1971-76. Up-
per Snake River Valley Hist. Soc., Box 244
Rexburg, 83440. Ed. Louis Clements. Indexed
at end of completed volume.

ILLINOIS

Central Illinois Historical Messenger
                              1969-   Q $1
     United Methodist Church Central Ill.
Conference Comm. on Archives and Hist. 211
N. Park St. Bloomington, 61701. Not indexed.

Chicago History
                              1945-   S-A $4.50
     Chicago Hist. Soc., 1615 N. Clark St.,
60614. Ed. Isabel Grossner. Annual index.
Indexed in Writings on American History, 1948-
America: History and Life, 1967-.

Chronicle
                              1970-   Q
     Macon Co. Hist. Soc., 1736 N. Main St.,
Decatur, 2526.

The Circuit Rider
                              1976-   Q $5
     Sangamon Co. Hist. Soc., Box 1829,
Springfield, 62701. Ed. Mrs. M. B. Menden-
hall. Index on cards.

Cobweb
                              1968-   M $5
     Des Plaines Hist. Soc., 777 Lee St., Des
Plaines, 60017. Ed. Richard W. Welch. Not
indexed.

Coles Historical Series
                         1974-   Q $7.50
        Coles Co. Hist. Soc., Charleston,
61920. Ed. Donald Tingley. Not indexed.

Crackerbarrel
                         1963-   B-M
        Elgin Area Hist. Soc., 444 Park St.,
Elgin, 60120.

Elsah History
                                 Q $3
        Historic Elsah Foundation, Elsah,
62028. Ed. Paul O. Williams.

Flagg Township Historical Society Bulletin
                         1968-   B-M $5
        921 N. 6th St., Rochelle, 61068. Ed.
Franklin Kruger.

Fountain Square Recalls
        Evanston Hist. Soc., 225 Greenwood Ave.
Evanston, 60201.

Frankfort Reflections
                         1972-   M $25
        Frankfort Area Hist. Soc. of Will Co.,
27 Ash St., Frankfort, 60423. Ed. Marie
Tenes. Not indexed.

Fulton County Historical Society Quarterly
Newsletter   1969-   Q $10
        45 N. Park Dr., Canton, 61520. Ed.
Curtis Strode. Not indexed.

Goshen Trails
                         1965-   Q $2
        Hamilton Co. Hist. Soc., 209 W. 1st. St.
Danville, 61832. Not indexed.

Hancock County Historical Society Newsletter
                         1968-   Q
        Not indexed.

Heritage of Vermilion County
                          1965-   Q
     Vermilion Co. Mus. Soc., 116 N. Gil-
Bert St., Danville, 61832. Not indexed.

Highland Park Historical Society Newsletter
                          1966-   8/yr. $3
     Box 56, Highland Park, 60035. Ed.
Henry X. Arenberg. Not indexed.

The Historical Messenger
                          1969-   Q $2
     Comm. on Archives and Hist., 1211 N.
Park St., Bloomington, 61701. Ed. L. W.
Turner. Not indexed.

Historically Speaking
     Waukegan Hist. Soc., 1917 N. Sheridan
Rd., Waukegan, 60085.

Illinois History
                          1947-   8/yr. $1.25
     Illinois State Hist. Soc., Old State
Capitol, Springfield, 62706. Annual index.
Cumulative index, 1947-72. Indexed in Sub-
ject Index to Children's Magazines.

Iroquois Stalker
                          1971-   Q $4.50
     Iroquois Co. Hist. Soc., Old Courthouse
103 W. Cherry St., Watseka, 60970. Ed. Mary
J. Miller. Annual index for v. 3.

Journal of the Illinois State Historical
Society   1908-   Q $12.50
     Old State Capitol, Springfield, 62706.
Ed. Ellen M. Whitney. Annual Index. Cumulative indexes, v. 1-25; 26-50; 51-60. Indexed
in Writings on American History, 1906-;
America: History and Life, 1964-; Abstracts
of English Studies, 1962, 1968, 1970-71,
1973; Abstracts of Folklore Studies, 1972.

Lombard Historical Society Newsletter
                    1971-   Q $5
     23 W. Maple St., Lombard, 61048. Ed.
Mary Perry. Not indexed.

Mocohisco News
                    1962-   M
     Monroe Co. Hist. Soc., Box 48, Water-
loo, 62298. Not indexed.

Moultrie County Heritage
                    1973-   Q $5
     Moultrie Co. Hist. and Genealogical
Soc., Box MM, Sullivan, 61951. Ed. Mrs.
Shirley Lynn. Annual index on cards.

Northern Historical Record
     Northern Illinois Hist. Soc., Box 50,
Grayslake, 60030.

The Prairie Historian
                    1971-   Q $5
     The Prairie Historians, Cole and Elm
Sts., Waltonville, 62894. Ed. Jerry H.
Elliston.

Samplers
     Marshall Co. Hist. Soc., 310 S. Prairie
St., Lacon, 61540.

Schuylerite
                    1972-   Q $5
     Schuyler-Brown Hist. Soc., Congress and
Madison Sts., Rushville, 62681. Eds. Lavina
Walton and Margaret Walker. Annual index.

Southmor Post
                    1963-76
     Illinois Valley Hist. Soc., Rt. 4,
Southmor Rd., Morris, 60450. No longer published.

Swedish Pioneer Historical Quarterly
                          1950-   Q $7
     5125 N. Spaulding Ave., Chicago, 60625.
Annual index. Cumulative index 1950-69.
Indexed in Writings on American History,
1950-; America: History and Life, 1963-.

Washingtonian
                          1968-   Q
     Hist. Soc. of Washington Co., Box 9,
Nashville, 62263. Not indexed.

What's In Zion
     Zion Hist. Soc., 1300 Shiloh Blvd.,
Zion, 60099.

Where the Trails Cross
                          1971-   Q $7
     South Suburban Genealogical and Hist.
Soc., 159th St., Bldg 1, South Holland, 60473.

                    INDIANA

Auburn-Dekalb Vanguard
                          1969-   Irreg. $2
     Vanguard Pub. Co., Box 347, Auburn,
46706. Not indexed.

Battlefield Bannar
      Battle Ground Hist. Corp., Box 225,
Aurora, 47920.

Circuit Writer
                          1963-   A   Free
     Roy O. West Library, DePauw Univ., Green-
castle, 46135. Not indexed.

Conner Prairie Peddler
                          1974-   B-M $10
     Conner Prairie Pioneer Settlement, 30
Conner Ln., Noblesville, 46060. Ed. Gus
Hardee. Not indexed.

Duneland Notes
                        1953-   M $1
        Duneland Hist. Soc., 411 Bowser Ave.,
Chesterton, 46304.   Ed. Norris D. Coambs. Not
indexed.

Fulton County Historical Society Quarterly
                        1964-   Q $5
        Race St., Rochester, 46975.   Ed. Shirley
Willard.   Cumulative index 1964-70 printed in
1971 issue.

Hendricks County History Bulletin
                        1967-   Q $3
        387 E. Broadway, Danville, 46118. Ed.
Margaret Baker.   Not indexed.

Henry County Historicalog
                        1972-   S-A $2
        Henry Co. Hist. Soc., 614 S. 14th St.,
New Castle, 47362.   Ed. Richard P. Ratcliff.
Nor indexed.

Historical Society Bulletin of Jasper County
        Jasper Co. Hist. Soc., 624 W. Clark St.
Rensselaer, 47978.

Indiana History Bulletin
                        1923-   M $1.50
        Indiana Hist. Bureau, State Library and
Hist. Bldg., 140 N. Senate Ave., Indianapolis, 46204.   Annual index.   Indexed in America: History and Life, 1968-.

Indiana Magazine of History
                        1905-   Q $5
        Indiana Hist. Soc., 140 N. Senate Ave.,
Indianapolis, 46204.   Cumulative index v. 1-
50/1905-54. The Indiana Div. of the Indiana
State Library maintains an index on cards for
this publication since 1954.   Indexed in Writings on American History, 1906-; Women Studies
Abstracts; America: History and Life, 1963-.

Leaves of Thyme
                              1949-   10/yr. $5
        Vigo Co. Hist. Soc., 1411 S. 6th St.,
Terre Haute, 47802. Ed. Juliet Peddle. Par-
tial indexing.

Madison County Historical Society Historical
Gazette   1967-   M $2
        Box 323, Anderson, 46015. Ed. Esther
Dittlinger. Not indexed.

Old Courthouse News
                              1967-   Q $5
        Northern Indiana Hist. Soc., 112 S. La-
fayette Blvd., South Bend, 46601. Ed. James
C. Sullivan. Not indexed.

Old Fort Bulletin
                              1931-   6/yr. $10
        Allen Co.-Fort Wayne Hist. Soc., 1424
W. Jefferson, Ft. Wayne, 46804. Ed. Gary G.
Ernest. Included in Index to Allen County-
Fort Wayne Historical Society Publications,
1967.

Old Fort News
                              1936-   Q
        Allen Co.-Ft. Wayne Hist. Soc., 1424
W. Jefferson, Ft. Wayne, 46804. Ed. Gary G.
Ernest. Included in Index to Allen County-
Ft. Wayne Historical Society Publications,
1967.

Weatenotes
                              1968-   10/yr. $4
        Tippecanoe Co. Hist. Assoc., 909 So.
St., Lafayette, 47901. Ed. Carol Waddell.
Not indexed.

Whitley County Historical Society Bulletin
                              1958-   B-M $3
        108 W. Jefferson St., Columbia City,
46725. Ed. Clean Fleck. Annual index.
Cumulative index 1958-72 in Dec., 1972 issue.

IOWA

Annals of Iowa
                         1893-   Q $1
     Iowa State Dept. of Hist. and Archives,
E. 12th St., Des Moines, 50319. Three indexes published, v. 1-8/1893-1909, v. 9-16/
1907-29, v. 17-28/1929-47. Since 1947 an
index appears in the final number of each
volume. Indexed in Writings on American
History, 1903-; America: History and Life,
1963-.

Bracket
     State Hist. Preservation Program, B-13
Maclean Hall, Univ. of Iowa, Iowa City,
52242.

Iowa Journal of History and Politics
                    1903-61
     Cumulative index, v. 1-40/1903-42.
Indexed in Writings on American History,
1906-.

Iowan
                         1952-   Q $8
     Shenandoah, 51601. Subject index on
cards, Iowa State Traveling Library, Des
Moines, Iowa.

Muscatine Area Heritage Review
     Muscatine Area Heritage Assoc., 705 W.
4th St., Muscatine, 52761.

Palimpsest
                    1920-   B-M
     State Hist. Soc. of Iowa, 402 Iowa Ave.,
Iowa City, 52240. Annual index. Cumulative
index, v. 1-20/1920-39. Indexed in Writings
on American History, 1920-; America: History
and Life, 1964-.

Trail Tales

                              1969-   Q $4
     Boone Co. Hist. Soc., 811 Keeler St.,
Boone, 50036. Ed. Edward H. Meyers. Not indexed.

Vignette

                              1964-   Q $3
     Iowa Co. Hist. Soc., Williamsburg,
52361. Ed. Harold R. Moore.

                        KANSAS

Heritage

                              1970-   Q $5
     Wichita Hist. Mus. Assoc., 3751 E.
Douglas Ave., Wichita, 67203. Ed. Robert
A. Pockett. Not indexed.

Kansas Historical Quarterly
                              1931-   Q $5
     Kansas State Hist. Soc., Memorial Bldg.,
120 W. 10th St., Topeka, 66612. Ed. Nyle
H. Miller. Thirty-six volumes are now
being indexed. Indexed in Writings on American History, 1931-; America: History and
Life, 1963-.

Leader Courier
     Kingman Co. Hist. Mus., Box 126, King-
man, 67068.

Our Yesteryears
                        1970-74
     Wilson Co. Hist Soc., Courthouse, Fre-
donia, 66736.

Shawnee County Historical Society Bulletin
                              1946-   Q $5
     Box 178, Topeka, 66601. Ed. J. W.
Ripley. Cumulative index, 1946-62.

KENTUCKY

Central Kentucky Researcher
                    1971-   M $5
     Taylor Co. Hist. Soc., Box 14, Camp-
bellsville, 42718. Not indexed.

Eastern Kentucky Historian
                    1966-   Q
     Research Historians, Rts. 23 and 460,
N., Paintsville, 41240.

Filson Club History Quarterly
                    1926-   Q $8
     Formerly The History Quarterly and
History Quarterly of the Filson Club.   The
Filson Club, 118 W. Breckinridge St., Louis-
ville, 40203. Ed. Nelson L. Dawson. Annual
index.   Indexed in Writings on American
History, 1929-; America: History and Life,
1970-.

Hart County Historical Society
                    1969-   Q $3
     502 N. Main St., Munfordville, 42765.
Ed. Dorothy J. Poore. Cumulative index.

Kentucky Ancestors
                    1965-   Q $5
     Kentucky Hist. Soc., Old State House,
Box H, Frankfort, 40601. Ed. Anne Fitz-
gerald. Not indexed.

Kentucky Pioneer
                    1968-   Q $2
     Madison Co. Hist. Soc., Inc., 120 W.
Main St., Richmond, 40475. Ed. James J.
Shannon, Jr. Not indexed.

Northern Kentucky Bulletin
                              1964-   Q
     Northern Kentucky Hist. Soc., Inc., 37
E. 4th St., Newport, 41071. Not indexed.

Register
                              1902-   Q $5
     Kentucky Hist. Soc., Old State House,
Box H, Frankfort, 40601. Ed. Hambleton Tapp.
Annual index. General index, 1902-45. In-
dexed in Writings on American History, 1906-;
America: History and Life, 1963-.

Timbered Tunnel Talk
                              1965-   M $4
     Kentucky Covered Bridge Assoc., Box 100,
Newport, 41072. Not indexed.

                    LOUISIANA

Attakapas Gazette
                              1965-   Q $5
     105 S. New Market St., Martinville,
70582. Ed. Carl Brasseaux. Annual index.

De Soto Plume
     DeSoto Hist. Soc., Box 523, Mansfield,
71052.

Foundation Flashes
                              1963-   B-M $25
     Found. for Hist. Louisiana, 900 N.
Blvd., Baton Rouge, 70802. Ed. Susan
McAdams. Not indexed.

Louisiana Historical Quarterly
                              1917-   Q
     Formerly its Publications, 1895-1917.
231 Carondelet St., New Orleans, 70130. Indexed in Writings on American History, 1917-;
Historical Abstracts, 1955-60.

Louisiana History
                          1960-   Q $7.50
      Louisiana Hist. Assoc., Box44422, Capitol
Station, Baton Rouge, 70804. Ed. Glenn R.
Conrad.   Annual index.   Cumulative index
planned.   Indexed in Writings on American
History, 1960, 1973-; Historical Abstracts,
1961-62; America: History and Life, 1963-;
Abstracts of English Studies, 1965-67, 1971.

North Louisiana Historical Association Journal
                          1969-   Q
      Louisiana Tech, Box 6008 Tech Station,
Rustin, 71270. Not indexed.

                    MAINE

Down East Magazine
                          1954-   10/yr. $6
      Camden, 04843. Ed. Duane Doolittle.
Cumulative index, 1954-65. Indexed at Fogler
Library, University of Maine, Orono.

Gray Matter
      Gray Hist. Soc., Gray, 04039.

The Landmarks Observer
                          1970-   B-M
      Greater Portland Landmarks, Inc., Box
4197, Station A, Portland, 94101. Cumulative
index on cards.

Maine Historical Society Quarterly
                          1961-   Q $15
      485 Congress St., Portland, 04111. Ed.
Gerald E. Morris.   Index on cards.

Musings
                          1969-72
      Maine State Mus. Comm., State House,
Augusta, 04330. Not indexed.

Old Mill News
                              1972-   Q $5
        Soc. for the Preservation of Old Mills,
    Box 435, Wiscasset, 04578. Ed. Donald W.
    Martin.

The Quarterdeck
                              1972-   Irreg.
        Olde Port Mus. Assoc., Portland, 04104.
    Not indexed.

                         MARYLAND

Along the Tow Path
        Chesapeake and Ohio Canal Assoc., Box
    66, Glen Echo, 20016.

Anne Arundel History Notes
                              1962-   Q
        Not indexed.

Carroll County Historical Society Newsletter
                              1952-   Q
        Not indexed.

Chronicles of St. Mary's
                              1952-   M
        St. Mary's Co. Hist. Soc., Box 212,
    Leonardtown, 20650. Not indexed.

Glades Star
                              1941-   Q
        Garrett Co. Hist. Soc., Center St.,
    Oakland, 21550. Not indexed.

Harford Heritage
        Hist. Soc. of Harford Co., Inc., Box
    391, Bel Air, 21014.

History Trails

                      1966-   Q $4
     Baltimore Co. Hist. Soc., 9811 Van Buren
Ln., Cockeysville, 21030. Not indexed.

Journal of the Alleghenies

                      1963-   A
     Council of the Alleghanies, Grantsville,
21536.

Maryland Historian

                      1970-   S-A $2
     Univ. of Maryland, Hist. Dept., College
Park, 20742. Indexed in America: History
and Life, 1970-.

Maryland Historical and Genealogical Bulletin

                      1930-50
     Annual index.

Maryland Historical Magazine

                      1906-   Q $10
     Maryland Hist. Soc., 201 W. Monument
St., Baltimore, 21201. A project to index
v. 1-50/1906-56 is nearing completion. This
index is on cards at the Maryland Hist. Soc.
Indexed in Writings on American History,
1906-; America; History and Life, 1963-.

The Montgomery County Story

                      1957-   Q $4
     Montgomery Co. Hist. Soc., 103 W. Mont-
gomery Ave., Rockville, 20850. Ed. Mary
Charlotte Crook. Not indexed.

The Record

     Hist. Soc. of Charles Co., Port Tobacco,
20677.

Steppingstones

     Steppingstones Mus. Assoc., Box 94A,
Street, 21154.

MASSACHUSETTS

Acorn
                            1965-   11/yr. $5
    Sandwich Hist. Soc. and Glass Mus., 129
Main St., Sandwich, 02563. Ed. Eleanor P.
Clarkson. Not indexed.

American Jewish Historical Quarterly
                            1893-   Q $15
    Formerly Jewish Historical Society Pub-
lications. Two Thornton Rd., Waltham, 02154.
Annual index. Cumulative index, v. 1-20. A
cumulative index, v. 21-50 is in preparation.
Indexed in Writings on American History,
1902-; Historical Abstracts, 1954-62; America: History and Life, 1963-.

American Neptune; A Quarterly Journal of Mari-
time History   1941-   Q $16
    Peabody Mus. of Salem, Salem, 01970.
Ed. Phillip C. F. Smith. Annual index.
Cumulative index every fifth year. Indexed
in Writings on American History, 1948-;
Historical Abstracts, 1957-62; America:
History and Life, 1963-; Abstracts of Eng-
lish Studies, 1961, 1971-.

Belmont Historical Society Newsletter
                                            $3
    Box 7, Belmont, 02178. Ed. Richard B.
Betts.

Berkshire History
                            1971-   Irreg. $2
    Berkshire Co. Hist. Soc., Inc., 113 E.
Housatonic St., Pittsfield, 01201.

Bostonian Society Proceedings
                              1881-   A $3
        206 Washington St., Boston, 02109. Ed.
W. M. Whitehill.   Cumulative index to 1932.
Indexed in Writings on American History,
1902-.

Bulletin for Johnny Cake Hill
                              1956-   Q
        Formerly The Navigator.   Old Dartmouth
Hist. Soc., Johnny Cake Hill, New Bedford,
02740.   Cumulative index.

Crosstaff and Astrolobe
                              1959-   Q
        Gosnold Soc. of Cape Cod, Inc., 702
Quaker Rd., North Falmouth, 02556.   Cumulative index.

The Dukes County Intelligencer
                              1959-   Q $5
        Dukes Co. Hist. Soc., Cooke and
School Sts., Edgartown, 02539.   Ed. Thomas
E. Norton.   Cumulative index, 1959-1972.

Essex Institute Historical Collections
                              1859-   Q $10
        Formerly Essex Antiquarian.   132 Essex
St., Salem, 01970.   Annual index.   Cumulative
index up to 1949 in preparation.   Indexed in
Writings on American History, 1902-; America:
History and Life, 1963-; Abstracts of Folk-
lore Studies, 1970-72.

Grapevine
                                    Irreg. $5
        Golden Ball Tavern Trust, Box 223,
Weston, 02193.   Not indexed.

Historic Nantucket
                                    Q $5
        Nantucket Hist. Assoc., Box 106, Old
Town Bldg., Nantucket, 02554.   Annual index.

Howland Quarterly
                                    1936-   Q
      Pilgrim John Howland Soc., Inc., Ply-
mouth, 02895. Not indexed.

Jackson Journal
                                    S-A $3
      Jackson Homestead, 527 Washington St.,
Newton, 02158. Ed. Betsy Allen. Not indexed.

Massachusetts Historical Society Proceedings
                              1859-   A $10
      1154 Boyleston St., Boston, 02215. Ed.
Malcolm Freiberg. Annual index. Cumulative
indexes, v. 1-20, 21-40, 41-60. Indexed in
Writings on American History, 1906-; Historical Abstracts, 1953-62; America: History
and Life, 1963-.

Middleborough Antiquarian
                              1959-   Q $3
      Middleborough Hist. Assoc., Box 272,
Middleboro, 02346. Ed. Mrs. Lawrence B.
Romaine. Cumulative index.

New England Galaxy
                              1959-   Q $4
      Old Sturbridge Village, 01566. Cumu-
lative index on cards.

New England Historical and Genealogical Register   1847-   Q $12.50
      New England Hist. and Genealogical Soc.,
101 Newbury St., Boston, 02116. Annual index. Cumulative index, v. 1-50/1847-96. Indexed in Writings on American History, 1902-.

News and Notes
                              1962-   B-M $5
      Berkshire Co. Hist. Soc., Inc., 780
Holmes Rd., Pittsfield, 01201. Ed. Donald
S. Smith. Not indexed.

News from the Congregational Christian Historical Society   1952-   3/yr. $2
        Wheaton College, Norton, 02766. Ed. H.
    F. Worthley. Not indexed.

Old Dartmouth Historical Sketches
                          1903-   Irreg.
        Old Dartmouth Hist. Soc., Johnny Cake
    Hill, New Bedford, 02740. Cumulative index
    on cards.

Old Time New England
                          1910-   Q $5
        Formerly The Bulletin. Soc. for the
    Preservation of New England Antiquities,
    141 Cambridge St., Boston, 02114. Annual
    index. Cumulative index on cards.

Quarterly News
                          1964-   Q $5
        Longyear Hist. Soc., 20 Seaver St.,
    Brookline, 02146. Ed. R. C. Molloy. Cumu-
    lative list of contents.

Rowe Historical Society Bulletin
                          1963-   Q $4
        Rowe Hist. Soc., Inc., Zoar Rd., Rowe,
    01367. Ed. Helen McCarthy. Not indexed.

Royall House Reporter
                          1961-   Irreg. $4
        Royall House Assoc., 15 George St.,
    Medford, 02155. Ed. F. D. Hall. Not indexed.

SRVHS Newsletter
                          1962-   3/yr. $1.50
        Swift River Hist. Soc., Inc., New Salem,
    01355. Ed. A. B. Bixby. Not indexed.

Scituate Historical Bulletin
        Scituate Hist. Soc., 121 Maple St.,
    Scituate, 02066.

Towpath Topics
                              1963-   Irreg. $4
     Middlesex Canal Assoc., Billerica,
01821. Ed. Arthur L. End, Jr. Not indexed.

Universalist Historical Society
                              1959-   Irreg. $5
     25 Beacon St., Boston, 02108. Ed.
James Hunt. Not indexed.

Weston Historical Society Bulletin
                              1963-   Q $2
     Box 343, Weston, 02193. Ed. Harold
Travio. Not indexed.

                    MICHIGAN

Bananza Bugle
     Lake Odessa Area Hist. Soc., Page
Bldg., 4th Ave., Lake Odessa, 48849.

Baraga Bulletin
                         1946-   Q $5
     Bishop Baraga Assoc., 239 Baraga
Ave., Marquette, 49855. Ed. Agnes B.
Rufus. Not indexed.

Chronicle
                         1965-   Q $6
     Hist. Soc. of Michigan, 2117 Washtenaw
Ave., Ann Arbor, 48104. Ed. Frank Wilhelme.
Indexed in Michigan Magazine Index, 1966-.

Dearborn Historian
                         1961-   Q   Free
     915 Brady St., Dearborn, 48124. Ed. W.
H. Arneson. Index to v. 1-5/1961-66, in
v. 5. Ten year cumulative index included in
last issue of 1970. Indexed in Michigan Magazine Index, 1966-.

Detroit Historical Society Bulletin
                    1945-
      5401 Woodward Ave., 48202. Cumula-
tive index, 1945-67. Indexed in Writings
on American History, 1948-; Michigan Magazine Index, 1966-.

Detroit in Perspective
                    1972-   3/yr.
      Detroit Hist. Soc., 5401 Woodward Ave.,
48202. Annual index, not printed.

Detroit Marine Historian
                    1946-   M
      Marine Hist. Soc. of Detroit, 43230.
Some annual indexes, quite irreg.

Grand Rapids Historical Society Newsletter
                    1901-   A $4
      Public Mus., 54 Jefferson, S. E.
Grand Rapids, 49502. Ed. Sharon Boisvenue.
Not indexed.

Harlow's Wooden Man
                              Q $3
      Marquette Co. Hist. Soc., 213 N. Front
St., Marquette, 49855. Ed. W. H. Treloar.
Society preparing index for significant
articles. Indexed in Michigan Magazine
Index, 1966-.

Macomb County Historical Society News Bulletin
                    1965-   M   5
      38775 By River Dr., Mount Clemens,
48043. Ed. Nancy M. McCain. Not indexed.

Mason Memories
      Mason Co. Hist. Soc., Inc., Box 1776,
Ludington, 49431.

Michigan History
                              1917-   Q $5
        Michigan Hist. Div., 208 N. Capitol
Ave., Lansing, 48933. Ed. Bartha Bigelow.
Cumulative index, 1917-62. Indexed in
Writings on American History, 1917-; Amer-
ica: History and Life, 1963-; Michigan
Magazine Index, 1966-.

Michigan Jewish History
                              1960-   3/yr. $10
        Jewish Hist. Soc. of Michigan, 163
Madison, Detroit, 48226. Ed. Irving Edgar.
Cumulative index, 1960-70 in v. 10, June,
1970. Indexed in Michigan Magazine Index,
1966-.

Midland Log
        Midland Co. Hist. Soc., 1801 W. St.
Andrews Dr., Midland, 48640.

Oakland Gazette
                              1968-   Q $6
        Oakland Co. Pioneer and Hist. Soc.,
405 Oakland Ave., Pontiac, 48016. Not indexed.

Up-to-date
                              1958-   Q $25
        Battle Creek Hist. Soc., 196 Capital
Ave., N. E., Battle Creek, 49017. Ed. Jean
Hunter. Not indexed.

Washtenaw Impressions
                              1970-   M $3
        Washtenaw Hist. Soc., 2708 Brockman
Blvd., Ann Arbor, 48104. Ed. Mrs. Lawrence
Ziegler. Not indexed.

MINNESOTA

Brown County's Heritage
     Hist. Mus., Broadway at First N., New
Ulm, 56073. Society maintains card file
index.

Goodhue County Historical News
                         1967-   3/yr. $1
     1166 Oak St., Red Wing, 55066. Ed. Mrs.
Milton Holst. Not indexed.

Happenings
                         1969-   M $10
     American Swedish Inst., 2600 Park Ave.,
Minneapolis, 55407. Ed. Wesley M. Wester-
berg. Not indexed.

Hennepin County History
                         1958-   Q $10
     2303 3rd Ave. S., Minneapolis, 55404.
Ed. B. C. Bensen. Cumulative index on cards.

Minnesota History
                         1915-   Q $6
     Minnesota Hist. Soc., 690 Cedar St.,
St. Paul, 55101. Index is published as a
separate. Indexed in Writings on American
History, 1915-; America: History and Life,
1963-; Abstracts of Folklore Studies, 1966-.

Morrison County Historical Society News and
Notes   1966-   M $2
     Box 239, Little Falls, Minnesota. Ed.
Jan Warner. Not indexed.

Over the Years
                         1961-   Q $2
     Dakota Co. Hist. Soc., Municipal Bldg.,
South St. Paul, 55075. Ed. A. B. Smeby.
Not indexed.

Polk County Historian
      213 E. Washington, Crookston, 56716.

Ramsey County History
      Ramsey Co. and St. Paul Hist. Soc., 75
W. 5th St., St. Paul, 55102.

Roots
                        1946-   3/yr. $4.50
      Formerly Gopher Historian.   Minnesota
Hist. Soc., 690 Cedar St., St. Paul, 55101.
Annual index.   Indexed in Abstracts of Folklore Studies, 1972; Subject Index to Children's Magazines.

Western Hennepin County Pioneers Association
News Bulletin   1968-   Q $5
      Long Lake, 55356.   Ed. R. A. Stubbs.
Cumulative index on cards.

                  MISSISSIPPI

Journal of Mississippi History
                        1939-   Q $6
      Mississippi Dept. of Archives and Hist.,
100 S. State St., Jackson, 39205.   Ed. John
E. Gonzales.   Cumulative index, v. 1-30/1939-
60, scheduled for completion by 1979.   Indexed in Writings on American History, 1939-;
America: History and Life, 1963-.

The Lumberjack
      Homochitto Valley Hist. Soc., Box 337,
Crosby, 39633.

Mississippi Coast Historical and Genealogical
Society Quarterly   1968-   Q $8
      Box 513, Biloxi, 39530.   Ed. Mrs. Julia
C. Guice.   Not indexed.

MISSOURI

Audrain County Historical Society. Newsletter
                    1965-   Q
    501 S. Muldrow, Mexico, 65265. Not
indexed.

Buck and Ball
                    1960-   10/yr
    Civil War Round Table of the Ozarks,
397 E. Central, Springfield, 65802. Not
indexed.

Bushwacker
                    1956-   8/yr. $22
    Civil War Round Table of St. Louis,
24 Log Cabin Dr., 63124. Not indexed.

Bushwacker
                    1966-   A $5
    Vernon Co. Hist. Soc., Route 1, Nevada,
64772. Ed. Patrick Brophy. Not indexed.

Camden County Historian
                    1969-72(?)
    Linn Creek, 65052. Not indexed.

Camden County Historical Society. Bulletin
                    1960-   Q
    103 Collier Lane, Fulton, 65251.

Carondelet Historical Society. Newsletter
                    1968-   Q
    3948 Federer Pl., St. Louis, 63116.
Not indexed.

Chariton County Historical Society. Newsletter
                    1967-   Q $5
    Salisbury, 65281. Ed. Jordan R.
Bentley. Not indexed.

Clay County Museum Association. Newsletter
                         1961(?)-   M
         Liberty, 64068. Not indexed.

DeKalb County Heritage
                         1970-   Q $5
         DeKalb Co. Hist. Soc., Maysville,
64469. Not indexed.

Florissant Valley Historical Society.   Quarterly
                         1959-   Q $2
         Florissant, 63031.   Ed. Mrs. Fred
Gladbach. Not indexed.

Historical Association of Greater Cape
Girardeau. Bulletin   1969-   B-M
         Cape Girardeau, 63701. Not indexed.

Jackson County Historical Society. Journal
                         1958-   Q
         217 N. Main St., Independence, 64050.
Not indexed.

Johnson County Historical Society. Bulletin
                         1960-   Q $4
         Main and   Gay, Warrensburg, 64093. Not
indexed.

Kingdom of Callaway Historical Society.
Bulletin.
         Fulton, 65251.

Kirkwood Historical Review
                         1962-   Q
         Kirkwood Hist. Soc., Kirkwood Br. P.O.
St. Louis, 63122. Cumulative index, v.1-
6/1962-67.

Landmarks Letter
                         1966-   Q
         Landmarks Assoc. of St. Louis, 304A
N. Euclid Ave., St. Louis, 63108. Ed. Jane
McCammon. Not indexed.

Lawrence County Historical Society. Bulletin
                    1961-   Q $2
        210 N. Main St., Mount Vernon, 65712.
    Ed. Fred G. Mieswinkel. Annual index.

Missouri Historical Review
                    1906-   Q
        State Hist. Soc. of Missouri,
    Hitt and Lowry Sts., Columbia, 65201.
    Ed. Richard S. Brownlee. Annual index.
    Cumulative index, 1906-51. Indexed in
    Writings on American History, 1906-;
    America: History and Life, 1963-; Women
    Studies Abstracts; Abstracts of Folklore
    Studies, 1966-.

Missouri Historical Society. Bulletin
                    1944-   Q $7.50
        Jefferson Memorial Bldg., Forest Park,
    63112. Annual index. Cumulative index, 1944-
    50. Indexed in America: History and Life,
    1963-; Writings on American History, 1949-.

Ozarker
                    1964-   Q $2
        Formerly Shannon County Historical
    Review. Shannon Co. Hist. Soc., Eminence,
    65466. Ed. Robert Lee. Not indexed.

Phoebe Apperson Hearst Historical Society.
Newsletter   1969-   Q
        St. Clair, 63077.

Pioneer Press
                    1966-   A
        Mercer Co. Hist. Soc., Princeton,
    64673. Not indexed.

Platte County Historical Society. Bulletin
                    1953-   Irreg.
        Parkville, 64152. Not indexed.

Pleasant Hill Historical Society. Newsletter
                    1971-   Q
        Pleasant Hill, 64080.

Pony Express Mail
                          1973-   M
        Pony Express Hist. Assoc., Inc., 1202
    Penn St., St. Joseph, 64502.

Ray County Mirror
                          1974-   Irreg. $2
        Ray Co. Hist. Soc., W. Royle, Rich-
    mond, 64085. Ed. Clara Chenault.

St. Charles County Historical Society. Quarterly News   1970-   Q
        St. Charles, 63301. Not indexed.

Saline County Historical Society. Newsletter
                          1969-   S-A
        Marshall, 65340. Not indexed.

Trail Guide
                          1955-   Q $2.50
        Kansas City Posse of the Westerners,
    1711 Concord Court, Kansas City, 64110.
    Ed. Payson Lowell. Cumulative index.

Westport Historical Society. Quarterly
                          1965-   Q
        23 Westport Sq., Kansas City, 64111.
    Annual index.

White River Valley Historical Quarterly
                          1961-   Q
        Point Lookout, 65726.

                       MONTANA

Montana, The Magazine of Western History
                          1951-   Q $10
        Formerly The Montana Magazine of History.
    N. Roberts, Helena, 59601. Ed. Vivian A.
    Paladin. Annual index. Cumulative index,
    1951-60. Indexed in Writings on American His-
    tory, 1951-; America: History and Life, 1963-.

NEBRASKA

Brownville Bulletin
                          1958-   Q $7
       Brownville Hist. Soc., Inc., Box 186,
   Brownville, 68321.   Ed. Don Carlile.

Historical News
                                           $3
       Adams Co. Hist. Soc., Box 102, Hastings,
   68901.   Ed. Dorothy Creigh.

Historical Review
       Chappell Chapter Hist. Soc., Box 321,
   Chappell, 69129.

Museum of the Fur Trade Quarterly
                          1965-   Q $3
       Mus. Assoc. of the American Frontier,
   Rt. 2, Box 18, Chadron, 69337.   Ed. Charles
   E. Hanson, Jr.   Cumulative index printed
   every four years.

Nebraska History
                          1918-   Q $3
       Formerly Nebraska State Historical Soc-
   iety Publications.   1500 "R" St., Lincoln,
   68508.   Ed. Marvin F. Kivett.   Annual index.
   Cumulative index, 1918-58.   Indexed in America: History and Life, 1963-; Writings on
   American History, 1919-; Abstracts of Folklore Studies, 1966, 1970, 1974.

Work Paper
                          1969-   3/yr.
       American Hist. Soc. of Germans from
   Russia.   Cumulative index being prepared.

Yester News
       Hastings Mus., Hwy. 281 at 14th St.,
   Hastings, 68901.

NEVADA

Back Trails
                              1971-   M
        Southern Nevada Hist. Soc., 2900
Capistrano Ave., Las Vegas, 89109. Not
indexed.

Nevada Highways and Parks Magazine
                                        $2.75
        Nevada State Highway Dept., Carson
City, 89701.

Nevada State Historical Society Quarterly
                              1907-   Q $5
        Formerly Nevada Historical Society.
Papers. Nevada State Hist. Soc., 1650 N.
Virginia St., Reno, 89502. Annual index,
1972-. Cumulative index, 1907-71. Indexed
in America: History and Life, 1963-; Writings on American History, 1911-.

Northeastern Nevada Historical Society Quarterly
                              1970-   Q $5
        Box 503, Elko, 89801. Ed. Howard
Hickson. Not indexed.

NEW HAMPSHIRE

Durham Historic Association. Newsletter
                              1967-   B-M $2
        Durham, 03824. Not indexed.

Excursion
                              1920-   A $2
        Sandwich Hist. Soc., Maple St., Center
Sandwich, 03227.

Historical New Hampshire
                              1946-   Q $10
     New Hampshire Hist. Soc., 30 Park St.,
Concord, 03301. Ed. R. S. Wallace. Cumulative index, v. 1-25/1944-70. Index main-
tained in the New Hampshire State Library.
Indexed in Writings on American History,
1948-; America: History and Life, 1963-.

                    NEW JERSEY

The Avalanche
        Clark Hist. Soc., c/o Mrs. Rosemary M.
Guzzo, 140 School St., Clark, 07066.

Batsto Gazette
                              1966-   Q $2
     Batsto Citizens Comm., Batsto R. D.,
Hammonton, 08037. Ed. Joseph Wilson.

Bergen County History
                              1970-   A $10
     Bergen Co. Hist. Soc., Box 61, River
Edge, 07661. Ed. Mrs. Claire K. Tholl.
Not indexed.

Bulletin of the Camden County Historical Society   1944-   S-A $5
        Park Blvd. and Euclid Ave., Camden,
08103. Ed. Howard R. Kemble. Not indexed.

Castle Lite
                              1927-   5/yr. $5
     Passaic Co. Hist. Soc., Box 1729.
Paterson, 07509. Not indexed.

Crossroads
                              1963-   9/yr. $2.50
     New Jersey Hist. Soc., 230 Broadway,
Newark, 07104. Not indexed.

Cumberland County Historical Society Newsletter
$5
     Box 16, Greenwich, 08323.

Gloucester County Historical Society Bulletin
                          1947-   Q $4
     58 N. Broad St., Woodbury, 08096.   Ed.
Mrs. Frances Shute.   Typewritten index, v.
1-9.

Green Heritage
     Monmouth Co. Park System, Box 326, Lin-
croft, 07738.

Heritage News
                          1956-   3/yr.
     Paramus Hist. and Preservation Soc.,
650 E. Glen Ave., Ridgewood, 07450.   Not indexed.

Historical Society of Haddonfield Bulletin
                          1958-   3/yr.
     343 King's Hwy. E., Haddonfield, 08033.
Not indexed.

Historical Trail
     Hist. Soc. of the Southern New Jersey
Annual Conf. of the United Methodist Church,
Pennington, 08534.

Howell Works Chronicle
                          1972-76 A
     Deserted Village at Allaire, Allaire,
07727.   Not indexed.

Hunterdon Historical Newsletter
                          1965-   3/yr. $5
     Hunterdon Co. Hist. Soc., 114 Main St.,
Flemington, 08822.   Ed. Mrs. H. Vaughn-Eames.
Not indexed.

League of Historical Societies of New Jersey
Bulletin   1966-   Q
     Box 43, Layton, 07851.

Livingston Historical Society Proceedings
                    1968-   Irreg.
        Box 220, Livingston, 07039. Not indexed.

Machaponix Journal
                    1969-   M
        Battleground Hist. Soc., Box 1776, Ten-
nent, 07763. Not indexed.

The Mercer Oak
        Mercer Co. Cultural and Heritage Comm.,
640 S. Broad St., Trenton, 08607.

Monmouth Historian
                    1972-   A $15
        Formerly Monmouth County Historical
Association Bulletin. 70 Court St., Free-
hold, 07728. Ed. Charles T. Lyle. Not indexed.

New Jersey Historical Commission Newsletter
                    1970-   10/yr. Free
        113 W. State St., Trenton, 08625. Ed.
Peggy Lewis. Cumulative index on cards.

New Jersey History
                    1845-   Q $10
        Formerly New Jersey Historical Society
Proceedings. 230 Broadway, Newark, 07140.

North Jersey Highlander
                    1957-   Q $4.50
        North Jersey Highlands Hist. Soc., Box
1, Newfoundland, 07435. Annual index. Cumulative index in preparation.

Passaic County Historical Society Bulletin
                    1927-   5/yr. $5
        Box 1729, Paterson, 07509. Ed. E. A.
Smyk.

Relics
                    1955-   5/yr. $3
        Pascack Hist. Soc., Box 285, Park
Ridge, 07675. Annual index.

Remembrances of Passaic County
                         1970-   Irreg. $5
     Lambert Castle, Paterson, 07503.   Ed.
E. A. Smyk.

Salem County Historical Society Newsletter
                         1968-   Q $3
     79-83 Market St., Salem, 08079.   Ed.
Robert Gardner.

The Towpath Post
                         1969-   Q $5
     Canal Soc. of New Jersey, Macculloch
Hall, Box 737, Morristown, 07960.   Ed. R.
R. Goller.   Not indexed.   Not published in
1972.

Turkey Tracks
                         1967-   Q   Free
     New Providence Hist. Soc., Box 661,
New Providence, 07974.   Ed. Mrs. R. Gorton.
Not indexed.

Ye Old Tye News
                         1967-   10/yr.
     350 W. Blackwell St., Dover, 07801.
Ed. Vivian Berg.   Not indexed.

NEW MEXICO

Greater Llano Estacado Southwest Heritage
                         1971-   Q $10
     Formerly Llano Estacado Heritage. Llano
Estacado Heritage, Inc., Box 2446, Hobbs,
88240.   Not indexed.

Historical News
                         1964-   Irreg.
     Taos Co. Hist. Soc., Inc., Box 398,
Taos, 87571.   Not indexed.

New   Mexico Historical Review
                              1926-   Q $6
        Univ. of New Mexico, Albuquerque, 87131.
Annual index.   Cumulative index, v. 1-15,
16-30, 31-45.   Indexed in Writings on American
History, 1926-; Historical Abstracts, 1954-
63; America: History and Life, 1963-.

Noticias Alagres de la Casa Kit Carson
                              1969-   Q $10
        Kit Carson Memorial Found., Inc., Old
Kit Carson Rd., Taos, 87571.   Ed. J. K.
Boyer.   Not indexed.

El Palacio
                              1913-   Q $6
        Mus. of New Mexico, Box 2087, Santa Fe,
87501.   Cumulative index in preparation,
1913-73.

Publications in History
        Socorro   Co. Hist. Soc., Inc., Box 923,
Socorro, 87801.

Rio Grande History
                              1973-   S-A $10
        Rio Grande Hist. Collections, Box 3475,
Las Cruces, 88003.   Ed. Austin Hoover.   Not
indexed.

                        NEW YORK

Albany Institute of History and Art   Bulletin
        125 Washington Ave., Albany, 12210.

Andaste Inquirer
                              1972-   Irreg. $2
        Corning Painted Post Hist. Soc., Box
104, Corning, 14830.   Ed. Richard Bessey.
Not indexed.

Annals and Recollections
    Rome Hist. Soc., 113 Court St., Rome,
13440.

Bronx County Historical Society Journal
                            1964-   S-A $15
    3266 Bainbridge Ave., N. Y. C., 10467.
Ed. Prof. Lloyd Ultan. Planning a cumulative
index, 1964-present.

Broome County Historical Society Bulletin
                                        Irreg.
    30 Front St., Binghamton, 13905. Cumu-
lative index, 1953-60.

Canals
    Canal Mus., Weighlock Bldg., Erie Blvd.,
E., Syracuse, 13202.

Chemung Historical Journal
                            1955-   Q
    Chemung Co. Hist. Soc., Inc., 304
William St., Elmira, 14901. Ed. Thomas E.
Byrne. Cumulative index, 1955-70.

Chester History Today
                            1962-   Q $2.50
    Hist. Soc. of the Town of Chester, Inc.,
Town Hall, Chestertown, 12817. Ed. Caroline
H. Fish. Not indexed.

Clarence Pioneer
    Hist. Soc. of the Town of Clarence.

Cohocton Journal
                            1973-   B-M $3
    Cohocton Hist. Soc., Rt. 1, Cohocton,
14826. Ed. Mrs. Marion Sauerbier.

Cuba Historical Society Newsletter
                            1970-   M
    Cuba Hist. Soc., 11 Grace St., Cuba,
14727.

De Halve Maen
                          1922-   Q $10
     Holland Soc. of New York, 122 E. 58th
St., N. Y. C., 10022. Ed. Richard H. Amer-
man. Cumulative index, 1922-59.

Drummer Boy
                                         $2.50
     Tappantown Hist. Soc., Box 71, Tappan,
10983. Ed. Rolf Korstvedt.

Enjine! Enjine!
                          1968-   Q $8
     Soc. for the Preservation and Apprecia-
tion of Antique Motor Fire Apparatus in
America, Inc., Box450, Eastwood Sta., Syracuse, 13206. Ed. Richard A. Horstmann. Not
indexed.

Fort Ticonderoga Museum Bulletin
                          1927-   Irreg.
     Ft. Ticonderoga Assoc., Box 390, Ticon-
deroga, 12833. Volume index.

Foundations; A Quarterly Journal of History and
Theology   1958-   Q $6
     Formerly The Chronicle. American Bap-
tist Hist. Soc., 1106 Goodman St., Rochester,
14620. Ed. Dr. Eldon G. Ernst. Annual index.

Franklin Historical Review
                          1964-   A $2
     Franklin Co. Hist. and Mus. Soc., 51
Milwaukee St., Malone, 12953. Ed. Elizabeth
Donovan. Not indexed.

Gates Gleanings
     Gates (Northampton) Heritage, 293 Youngs
Ave., Gates, 14606.

Genessee County Historical Federation Newsletter
                          1959-   Irreg.
     657 East Ave., Rochester, 14607. Not
indexed.

Genessee Country Scrapbook
      Rochester Hist. Soc., 485 East Ave.,
   Rochester, 14607.

Grist Mill
                        1967-   Q $5
      Saratoga Co. Hist. Soc., Box 426, Ball-
   ston Spa, 12020. Ed. Eleonor Grose. Not
   indexed.

Historic Comment
                        1965-   Q
      St. Lawrence Co. Hist. Center, Box 506,
   Canton, 13617.

Historic Ithaca Newsletter
                        1969-   Q $7.50
      Hist. Ithaca and Tompkins Co., Inc.,
   Box 151, Ithaca, 14850. Ed. Carol U. Sisler.

Historical Records and Studies
                        1899-   Irreg. $10
      United State Catholic Hist. Soc., St.
   Joseph's Seminary, Seminary Ave., Yonkers,
   10704. Ed. Rev. Thomas J. Shelley.

Horse Ocean
                        1971-   Q
      Canal Mus., Weighlock Bldg., Erie Blvd.,
   Syracuse, 13202. Not indexed.

Huguenot Historical Society Yearbook
                        1952-   A $5
      Huguenot Hist. Soc., Box 339, New Paltz,
   12561. Annual index. Cumulative index,
   1952-74 on cards.

Information Window
                                 Q $2
      Wantagh Preservation Soc., Box 132,
   Wantagh, 11793. Ed. Mrs. Anita Rofrano.
   Not indexed.

Intelligencer
      Ossining Hist. Soc. Mus.   Indexed in
Writings on American History, 1960.

Jefferson County Historical Society Bulletin
                        1961-   Q $10
      228 Washington St., Watertown, 13601.
Not indexed.

John Thurman Historical Society Quarterly
                        1963-   Q $3
      Athol, 12810.   Not indexed.

Journal of Long Island History
                        1961-   S-A $6
      Long Island Hist. Soc., 128 Pierrepont
St., Brooklyn, 11201.   Ed. Everett Ortner.
Indexed in America: History and Life, 1963-.

Landmark Society Newsletter
                        1963-   B-M
      Landmark Soc. of Western New York, 130
Spring St., Rochester, 14608.

Lewis County Historical Society Journal
      Box 286, Lowville, 13367.   Ed. A. Ein-
horn.

Lumber Shover
                        1968-   M
      Hist. Soc. of the Tonawandas, Inc.,
113 Main St., Tonawanda, 14150.

Mohawk Valley Museum News Letter
                        1972-   M $5
      Formerly Comet.   Junior Mus. of Oneida
Co., 1703 Oneida St., Utica, 13501.   Ed.
Eino Kivisalu.

Nassau County Historical Journal
                        1942- $5
      Nassau Co. Hist. Soc., Box 207, Garden
City, 11530.   Ed. Dr. Myron H. Luke.   Cumulative index, 1942-52.

New York Historical Society Quarterly
                          1917-   Q $10
     New York Hist. Soc., 170 Central Park
W., N. Y. C., 10024.   Ed. Kathleen Luhrs.
Annual index.   Cumulative index, 1917-38,
typewritten.   Indexed in Writings on Amer-
ican History, 1917-; America: History and
Life, 1963-; Women Studies Abstracts.

New York History Quarterly
                          1919-   Q $12
     Formerly New York State Historical
Association Journal.   New York State Hist.
Assoc., Lake Rd., Cooperstown, 13326.   Ed.
Wendell Tripp.   Annual index.   Cumulative
index every 10 years.   Cumulative index,
v. 1-46/1919-65 in 5 v.   Indexed in Writ-
ings on American History, 1920-; Historical
Abstracts, 1955-62; America: History and
Life, 1963-; Abstracts of Folklore Stud-
ies, 1972.

Niagara Frontier
                          1953-   Q $8
     Buffalo and Erie Co. Hist. Soc., 25
Nottingham Ct., Buffalo, 14216.   Ed. Walter
S. Dunn, Jr.   Annual index.   Cumulative in-
dex.

North Country Notes
                          1960-   10/yr. $4
     Clinton Co. Hist. Assoc., City Hall,
Plattsburgh, 12901.   Cumulative topical indexes, 1960-68, 1969-71.

North Hempstead Antiquity
                          1968-   Irreg.
     Hist. Soc. of the Town of North Hemp-
stead, 220 Plandone Rd., Manhasset, 11031.
Not indexed.

North River Navigator
                      1971-   M $10
        Hudson River Sloop Restoration, Inc.,
88 Market St., Poughkeepsie, 12601. Ed. Pat
McLaughlin.

Oniota
                      1967-   M
        318 Genessee St., Utica, 13502.

Oswego County Historical Society Journal
                      1937-   A
        Oswego Co. Hist. Soc., Richardson-Bates
House, 135 E. 3rd St., Oswego, 13126. Annual
index. Cumulative index, 1939-70 on cards.

Packet
                                         $5
        Saratoga Co. Hist. Soc., Box 426, Ball-
ston Spa, 12021. Ed. Kathleen S. Jarvis.

Placid Pioneer
        Lake Placid-North Elba Hist. Soc., 30
Lakeview St., Lake Placid, 12946.

Preservation Notes
                      1965-   3/yr. $10
        Soc. for the Preservation of Long Island
Antiquities, Box 206, Setauket, 11733. Ed.
Mrs. Barbara Ferris Van Liew. Cumulative in-
dex every three years.

Quarterly of the Historical Society of the Town
of Minerva   1971-   Q $2
        Minerva, 12851. Ed. Mrs. Clarence E.
Jones. Annual index.

Record
                      1870-   Q $10
        New York Genealogical and Biographical
Soc., 122 E. 58th St., N. Y. C., 10022. Ed.
Mrs. William R. White. Annual index. Cumulative index, v. 1-38. Indexed in Writings
on American History, 1902-.

Rochester History
                              1939-   Q $.50
       Rochester Public Library, 115 South
Ave., Rochester, 14604. Ed. Joseph W. Barnes.
Annual scope note in Historical Abstracts.

St. Lawrence County Historical Association
Quarterly   1956-   Q $10
       Box 8, Canton, 13617. Ed. Elsie Tyler.
Cumulative index, 1956-67.

Schenectady County Historical Society Newsletter
                              1965-   M
       32 Washington Ave., Schenectady, 12305.
Not indexed.

Schoharie County Historical Review
                                             $2.50
       Schoharie Co. Hist. Soc., Old Stone Ft.
Mus., N. Main St., Schoharie, 12157. Ed.
Mary Van Order Norton.

Schuyler County Historical Society Journal
                              1964-   Q $5
       Box 116, Montour Falls, 14865. Ed.
Barbara Bell. Annual index. Cumulative index.

Seaford Historical Society Quarterly
                              1970-   Q
       2234 Jackson Ave., Seaford, 11783. Not
indexed.

South of the Mountains
                              1957-   Q $5
       Hist. Soc. of Rockland Co., Kings Hwy.,
Orangeburg, 10962. Ed. M. Campbell.

Southold Historical Society and Museum Newsletter   1970-   A
       Southold Hist. Soc., Box 1, Southold,
11971. Not indexed.

Staten Island Historian

1938-   Q $4

  Staten Island Hist. Soc., 302 Center St.,
Staten Island, 10306.   Ed. Harlow McMillen.
Cumulative index, 1938-69.

Steamboat Bill

1940-   Q $5

  Steamship Hist. Soc. of America, Inc.,
414 Pelton Ave., Staten Island, 10310.   Ed.
Peter T. Eisele.   Annual index.   Cumulative
index, 1940-74.   Indexed in Writings on American History, 1949-60.

Then and Now

1968-   Q

  Formerly Canal Days.   Delaware and Hudson Canal Hist. Soc., High Falls, 12440.
Not indexed.

Three Village Historian

1965-   Irreg. $5

  Three Village Hist. Soc., Box 965, Stony
Brook, 11790.   Ed. Peter L. Bailey, Jr.   Not
indexed.

W. K. Vanderbilt Historical Society Newsletter
  Formerly Adelphi Historical Society Newsletter.   W. K. Vanderbilt Hist. Soc. of Dow-
ling College, Box 433, Oakdale, 11769.

Westchester Historian

1925-   Q $6

  Formerly Quarterly Bulletin.   Westchester Co. Hist. Soc., 43 Read Ave., Tuck-
ahoe, 10707.   Ed. R. Hoffman.   Separate
printed index every 10 years.

Ye Olde Alleganian

Irreg $2

  Allegany Co. Hist. Soc., 20 Willets
Ave., Belmont, 14813.   Ed. Bill Greene, Jr.

NORTH CAROLINA

Carolina Comments
                              1952-   B-M $2
     Div. of Archives and Hist., North Caro-
lina Dept. of Cultural Resources, 109 E.
Jones St., Raleigh, 27611. Ed. Mrs. Memory
F. Mitchell. Annual index.

Chronicle
     Bertie Co. Hist. Assoc., River St., Box
223, Colerain, 27924.

The Greensboro Historical Museum Journal
                              1974-   Q $5
     Greensboro Hist. Mus., 130 Summit Ave.,
Greensboro, 27401. Not indexed.

Historic Edenton, Inc.
     Cupola House Assoc., 105 N. Granville
St., Edenton, 27932.

Historical Foundation News
                              1944-   Q $2
     Hist. Found. of the Presbyterian and
Reformed Churches, Box 847, Montreat, 28757.
Ed. K. J. Foreman. Annual index. Cumu-
lative index in preparation.

Lower Cape Fear Historical Society Bulletin
                              1957-   3/yr. $8
     Box 813, Wilmington, 28401. Ed. Alan
D. Watson. Index on cards at Wilington
Public Library.

Mayflower News
     Soc. of Mayflower, 204 Hillcrest Dr.,
High Point, 27262.

Methodist History
                              1962-   Q $5
        Comm. on Archives and Hist. of the
United Methodist Church, Box 488, Lake Juna-
luska, 28745.   Annual index.

North Carolina Historical Review
                              1924-   Q $6
        North Carolina Office of Archives and
Hist., 109 E. Jones St., Raleigh, 27611.
Annual index.   Cumulative index, 1924-63.
Cumulative index, 1924-74 in preparation.
Indexed in Writings on American History,
1926-; America: History and Life, 1963-.

Old Salem Gleaner
                              1957-   Q $10
        Old Salem, Inc., Old Salem Rd., Drawer F,
Salem Sta., Winston-Salem, 27108.   Not indexed.

Perquimans County Historical Society Yearbook
                                      A $3
        Box 285, Hertford, 27944.   Ed. Raymond
A. Winslow.

Stanly County Early History
        Stanly Co. Hist. Soc., 813 W. Main St.,
Albemarle, 28001.

                      NORTH DAKOTA

North Dakota History; Journal of the Northern
Plains   1906-   Q $5.20
        Formerly North Dakota Historical Quarter-
ly.   State Hist. Soc. of North Dakota, Li-
berty Memorial Bldg., Bismarck, 58501.   Ed.
Larry Remele.   Cumulative index, 1906-70.
Indexed in Writings on American History,
1908-; America: History and Life, 1963-.

North Dakota Quarterly
>1910-   Q $5
>   Univ. of North Dakota, Grand Forks,
58201. Cumulative index, v. 1-15/1910-25 in
v. 16. Indexed in America: History and Life,
1963-.

Plains Talk
>1963-   Q
>   State Hist. Soc. of North Dakota, Li-
berty Memorial Bldg., Bismarck, 58501. Ed.
Larry Remele.

Red River Historian
>1966-   Q $10
>   Red River Valley Hist. Soc., Minard Hall,
North Dakota State Univ., Fargo, 58102. Eds.
A. Gordon Pruden and Sister Bertha Hill.
Not indexed.

Steele County Historical Notes
>   Hope, 58046.

Trails and Smoke Signals
>1967-   Q $2
>   North Dakota Hist. Soc., Inc., Cole-
harbor, 58531. Ed. Dave Robinson. Not indexed.

Walsh Historical News
>   Walsh Co. Hist. Soc., Minto, 58261.

Wells County History
>1969-   M $2
>   Wells Co. Hist. Soc., Inc., Sykeston,
58426. Cumulative index on cards.

OHIO

Allen County Reporter

                        1943-   Q $5
       Formerly The Reporter. Allen Co. Hist.
Soc., 620 W. Market St., Lima, 45801. Annual
index.

Black Swamp Chanticleer

                        1955-   M $2
       Wood Co. Hist. Soc., 301 Sand Ridge Rd.,
Bowling Green, 43402. Ed. Lyle R. Fletcher.
Not indexed.

The Canawler

                        1968-   S-A $15
       Canal Fulton Heritage Soc., Box 607,
Canal Fulton, 44614. Ed. Joetta Brownfield.
Not indexed.

Cincinnati Historical Society Bulletin

                                         $25
       Eden Park, 45202. Ed. Mrs. Dottie
Lewis. Indexed in America: History and Life,
1963-.

Clark County Historical Society Newsletter

                        1971-   M $5
       300 W. Main St., Memorial Hall,
Springfield, 45504. Not indexed.

Defiance Heritage

                        1966-   A
       Defiance Co. Hist. Soc., Box 801,
Defiance, 43512. Not indexed.

Echoes

                        1928-   M $5
       Ohio Hist. Soc., Hist. Center, Columbus,
43211. Ed. J. Richards.

Flashback
                              1967-72 3/yr.
        Hudson Library and Hist. Soc., 22
Aurora St., Hudson, 44236.

Flint Stones
        Western Columbiana Co. Hist. Soc.,
Homeworth Alliance Rd., Homeworth, 44634.

Four County Crossroads
        Bellevue Area Hist. Soc., Box 304,
Bellevue, 44811.

Geauga County Historical Society Quarterly
                         1961-   Q $5
        Box 153, Burton, 44021. Ed. Richard
R. Berg. Not indexed.

Hardin County Museum Bulletin
        Hardin County Archeological and Hist.
Soc., 327 N. Main St., Kenton, 43266.

Historicalog
                         1943-   M $5
        Warren Co. Hist. Soc., Lebanon, 45306.
Ed. Elva R. Adams. Not indexed.

Inland Seas
                         1945-   Q $7.50
        Great Lakes Hist. Soc., 480 Main St.,
Vermelion, 44089. Annual index. Indexed in
Writings on American History, 1948-; America:
History and Life, 1963-; Peace Research Ab-
stracts Journal; Michigan Magazine Index.

Intelligencer
                                  M $2
        Worthington Hist. Soc., High St.,
Worthington, 43085. Ed. Mildred J. Plapp.
Not indexed.

Ionic Columns
                        1968-   10/yr. $10
        Montgomery Co. Hist. Soc., Old Court
House, Dayton, 45402. Ed. Jeanne R. Palermo.
Not indexed.

Lake County Historical Society Quarterly
                        1959-   Q $5
        8095 Mentor Ave., Mentor, 44060.   Index
of names, 1959-71.

Monographs of the Harrison County Historical
Society   1970-   A
        Park Ave., Cadiz, 43907. Not indexed.

Northwest Ohio Quarterly
                        1929-   Q $6
        Maumee Valley Hist. Soc., Wolcott House
Mus., 1031 River Rd., Maumee, 43537. Ed.
Dr. Richard J. Wright. Indexed in America:
History and Life, 1963-.

Ohio History
                        1887-   Q $10
        Formerly Ohio Historical Quarterly,
1887-1934; Ohio Archaeological and Historical
Quarterly. Ohio Hist. Soc., Columbus, 43211.
Ed. Dr. Thomas H. Hartig. Annual index.
Cumulative index, v. 1-20. Indexed in Writ-
ings on American History, 1903-: Historical
Abstracts, 1958-63; America: History and
Life, 1964-; Bibliographic Index, 1943-.

Old Portage Trail Review
                        1942-   Irreg.
        Formerly Summit County Historical Society
Bulletin. 500 Copley Rd., Akron, 44320. Not
indexed.

Our Heritage
        Greene Co. Hist. Soc., Church St.,
Xenia, 45385.

Pathways of the Pioneers
        Lorain Co. Hist. Soc., 509 Washington
    Ave., Elyria, 44035.

Pickaway Quarterly
                            1961-   Q $7.50
        Pickaway Co. Hist. Soc., Box 85, Circle-
    ville, 43113. Cumulative index covering
    1961-71 in progress.

Pioneer
        Afro-American Cultural and Hist. Soc.,
    Hist. Mus., 8716 Harkness Rd., Cleveland,
    44106.

Rombach Place Recorder
                            1969-   B-M $6
        Clinton Co. Hist. Soc., Box 529, Wilm-
    ington, 45177. Not indexed.

Semaphore
                            1968-   M $6
        Conneaut Hist. Railroad Mus., Box 643,
    Conneaut, 44030. Ed. Paul W. Prescott. Not
    indexed.

Sights and Sounds of Cosi
        Franklin Co. Hist. Soc., 280 E. Broad
    St., Columbus, 43215.

Surveyor
        Anderson Township Hist. Soc., 1481 Sutton
    Ave., Box 30174, Cincinnati, 54230.

Tallow Light
                            1966-   Q $5
        Washington Co. Hist. Soc., 401 Aurora
    St., Marietta, 45750. Ed. Owen P. Hawley.

Wellsville Echoes
        Wellsville Hist. Soc., 711 Riverside
    Ave., Wellsville, 43968.

Western Reserve Historical Society News
                        1946-   M $15
      10825 E. Blvd., Cleveland, 44106.   Ed.
   Kermit J. Pike. Cumulative index on cards,
   1946-55.

Western Reserve Magazine
                        1973-   B-M $7.50
      Box 243, Garrettsville, 44231. Ed. Mary
   Folger.

                    OKLAHOMA

American Scene
                        1958-   Q $7
      Thomas Gilcrease Inst. of American Hist.
   and Art, 2500 W. Newton, Tulsa, 74127. Not
   indexed.

Canadian County Historical Society Bulletin
                        1971-   A $5
      400 S. 10th St., Yukon, 73099. Ed. H.
   M. Woods. Not indexed.

The Chronicles of Oklahoma
                        1921-   Q $5
      Oklahoma Hist. Soc., Historical Bldg.,
   Oklahoma City, 43105. Ed. Kenny A. Franks.
   Annual index. Cumulative index, 1921-59.
   Indexed in Writings on American History,
   1921-.

Five Civilized Tribes Museum Newsletter
                                           $5
      Agency Hill, Honor Heights Dr., Musko-
   gee, 74401.

Five Tribes Journal
                        1975-   M $10
      Five Civilized Tribes Found., Musko-
   gee, 74401.

Great Plains Journal
                              1961-   S-A $3
     Mus. of the Great Plains, Box 68, Law-
ton, 73501. Cumulative index, 1961-72. Indexed in Historical Abstracts, 1961-62;
America: History and Life, 1963-; Abstracts
in Anthropology, 1970-.

The Heritage Hills News-Herald
     Heritage Hills Hist. Preservation, 311
N. W. 19th St., Oklahoma City, 73103.

The Oklahoma Baptist Chronicle
                              1958-   S-A $2
     Oklahoma Baptist Hist. Soc., Oklahoma
Baptist Univ., Shawnee, 74801. Ed. J. M.
Gaskin. Cumulative index every 5 years.

Oklahoma Heritage
     Oklahoma Heritage Assoc., 201 N. W. 14th
St., Oklahoma City, 73103.

Persimmon Hill
                              1970-   Q $6
     National Cowboy Hall of Fame and Western
Heritage Center, 1700 N. E. 63rd St., Oklahoma City, 73111. Not indexed.

Pontotoc County Quarterly
                              1969-   Q $4
     Pontotoc Co. Hist. and Genealogical Soc.,
Box 1646, Ada, 74820. Ed. Mrs. Virginia Har-
bin. Not indexed.

Prairie Lore
                              1964-   Q $4
     Southwestern Oklahoma Hist. Soc., 916½
B Ave., Lawton, 73501.

Red River Valley Historical Review
                                      Q $15
     Red River Valley Hist. Assoc., Library
Suite 203, Southeastern State College, Dur-
ant, 74701.

OREGON

Columbia County History
                    1962-   A
        Columbia Co. Hist. Soc., 45 S. 21st St.,
    St. Helens, 97051. Annual index.

Crook County Historical Society Newsletter
                    1972-   Irreg.
        Bowman Mus., Prineville, 97754. Not
    indexed.

Curry County Historical Society Monthly Bulletin   1974-   M
        Not indexed.

Discovery
                    1974-   Q
        Northwest Trailblazers, Oregon Hist.
    Soc., 1230 S. W. Park Ave., Portland, 97205.
    Not indexed.

Finam Newsletter
                    1964-   Irreg.
        Finnish American Hist. Soc. of the West,
    130 N. W. 19th Ave., Portland, 97208. Not
    indexed.

Historically Speaking
        Polk Co. Hist. Soc., Dallas, 97338.

Klamath County Museum Research Papers
                    1959-   Irreg.
        1451 Main St., Klamath Falls, 97601.
    Not indexed.

Klamath Echoes
                    1964-   A
        1451 Main St., Klamath Falls, 97601.
    Not indexed.

Lane County Historian
                         1956-   Irreg.
     Lane Co. Pioneer Hist. Soc., 740 W. 13th
Ave., Eugene, 97402. Cumulative index, v. 1-
6/1956-61. Cumulative index, 1956-74 on
cards.

Marion County History
                         1955-   Irreg.
     Marion Co. Hist. Soc., Box 847, Salem,
97308. Indexed in Writings on American History, 1955-.

Old Church Organ
                         1968-   Q
     Old Church Soc., Inc., 1422 S. W. 11th
Ave., Portland, 97201. Not indexed.

Old Portland Today
                         1973-   M
     Hist. Outlet Center, Portland. Not in-
dexed.

Old Timer Newsletter
                         1966-   Irreg.
     Josephine Co. Hist. Soc., Kerby, 97526.
Not indexed.

Oregon Historical Quarterly
                         1900-   Q $10
     Formerly Quarterly of the Oregon Hist-
orical Society. Oregon Hist. Soc., 1230 S.
W. Park Ave., Portland, 97205. Annual index.
Cumulative index, 1900-39, 1940-60. Indexed
in Writings on American History, 1902-;
Historical Abstracts, 1955-62; America:
History and Life, 1963-; Women Studies Ab-
stracts.

Portland Friends of Cast Iron Architecture
Newsletter   1973-   Irreg.
     1030 S. W. 2nd Ave., Portland, 97204.
Not indexed.

Quarterdeck Review
                        1973-   Q
        Columbia River Maritime Mus., 16th and
Exchange Sts., Astoria, 97103. Not indexed.

Sponsorscoop
                        1974-   B-M
        Northwest Trailblazers, Oregon Hist.
Soc., 1230 S. W. Park Ave., Portland, 97205.

Trolley Park News
                        1959-   Irreg.
        Oregon Electric Railway Hist. Soc., Inc.,
Star Rt., Box 1318, Glenwood, 97120. Not indexed.

Umpqua Trapper
                        1965-   Q
        Douglas Co. Hist. Soc., Rt. 2, Box 759,
Roseburg, 97470. Annual index. Cumulative
index, 1965-73.

                     PENNSYLVANIA

Alle Kiska Historia
                                          $5
        Allegheny Kiski Valley Hist. Soc., Inc.,
Lock St., Tarentum, 15084. Ed. M. E. Carlson.

American Catholic Historical Society of Philadelphia Records   1886-   Q $10
        Box 84, 19105. Ed. Rev. John B. DeMayo.
   Indexed in Writings on American History,
   1902-; Historical Abstracts, 1954-62;
   America: History and Life, 1963-.

Bucks County Historical Society Journal
                        1972-   S-A $10
        Pine and Ashland Sts., Doylestown, 18901.

Canal Currents
                              1967-   Q
     Pennsylvania Canal Soc., c/o Earl B.
Giles, 818 Belmont Ave., Johnstown, 15904.
Cumulative index, 1967-71, not printed.

Casselman Chronicle
                        A $3
     Springs Hist. Soc. of The Casselman
Valley, Spring, 15562. Ed. A. E. Schrock.

Centre County Heritage
                         1957-   S-A $3
     Centre Co. Hist. Soc., Houserville Rd.,
State College, 16801. Ed. J. Marvin Lee.
Not indexed.

Columbian
                                   Irreg. $2
     Columbia Co. Hist. Soc., Box 105,
Bloomsburg State College, Bloomsburg, 17815.
Not indexed.

Community Historians of Lancaster County
Bulletin   5/yr. $3
     2215 Millstream Rd., Lancaster, 17602.
Ed. Dorcas Kriz.

Elk Horn
                         1965-   Q $3
     Elk Co. Hist. Soc., Box 361, Ridgway,
15863. Cumulative index in preparation.

Goschenhoppen Region
                         1965-   Q
     Goschenhoppen Historians, Inc., Woxall,
18979.

Historian
                         1959-71 Q
     Bucks Co. Hist. Soc., Pine and Ashland
Sts., Doylestown, 18901. Cumulative index,
1959-71.

Historic Bethlehem Inc. Newsletter
                    1961-   Q $10
     Main and Church Sts., 18018. Ed. Joan
Lardner Ward. Not indexed.

Historic Schaefferstown Record
                    1967-   Q
     Schaefferstown, 17088. Not indexed.

Historical Review of Berks County
                    1935-   Q $5
     Hist. Soc. of Berks Co., 940 Centre Ave.,
Reading, 19601. Annual index. Indexed in
Writings on American History, 1948-.

Historical Society of Fort Washington Monthly
                    1970-   M $5
     473 Bethlehem Pike, Ft. Washington,
19034. Ed. George Baker.

Lancaster County Historical Society Journal
                    1896-   Q $10
     230 N. President Ave., Lancaster, 17603.
Ed. John Ward Willson Loose. Indexed in
Writings on American History, 1902-.

Leaflet
                              Q $2
     Columbia Co. Hist. Soc., Bloomsburg
State College, Bloomsburg, 17815. Ed. Craig
A. Newton.

Lehigh County Historical Society Proceedings
                                       $7.50
     414 Walnut St., Allentown, 18102. Ed.
Dr. Donald B. Hoffman. Indexed in Writings
on American History, 1952, 1955-56, 1960.

Lycoming County Historical Society Journal
                    1919-   S-A
     Formerly Proceedings and Papers. 858
W. 4th St., Williamsport, 17701. Cumulative
index, 1955-73.

Mennonite Research Journal
                          1960-   Q $2.50
        Lancaster Mennonite Conference Hist.
Soc., 2215 Mill Stream Rd., Lancaster, 17602.
Cumulative index, 1960-69.

Mercer County History
                          1971-   S-A
        Mercer Co. Hist. Soc., 119 Pitt St.,
Mercer, 16137. Not indexed.

Mirror
                                             $5
        Lancaster Mennonite Conference Hist.
Soc., 2215 Mill Stream Rd., Lancaster, 17602.

Moravian Historical Society Transactions
                          1858-   S-A $3
        210 E. Center St., Nazareth, 18064.
Annual index. Cumulative index, 1858-1973.
Indexed in America: History and Life, 1963-.

News for Members
                          1966-   M
        Pittsburgh Hist. and Landmarks Found.,
Old Post Office, Pittsburgh, 15212. Not
indexed.

Northumberland County Historical Society
Proceedings   1906- $4
        1019 Susquehanna Ave., Sunbury, 17801.
Ed. Charles Fisher Snyder. Cumulative in-
dexes, 1908-46, 1947, 1949-63.

Now and Then
                          1868-   Q $4
        Muncy Hist. Soc., 44 N. Main St.,
Muncy, 17756. Ed. Dr. Eugene P. Bertin.
Indexed every 3 years.

Old York Road Historical Society Bulletin
                              1937-   A $3
      c/o Abington Library, Old York Rd.,
Jenkintown, 19046. Ed. Mrs. Warren Hilton.
Indexed in Writings on American History,
1937-.

Pennsylvania Dutch News and Views
                              1969-   S-A $4
      Formerly Rumlaefer. Pennsylvania Dutch
Folk Culture Soc., Inc., Lenhartville,
19534. Not indexed.

Pennsylvania History
                              1933-   Q $8
      Pennsylvania Hist. Assoc., Sparks Bldg.,
University Park, 16802. Ed. Dr. H. Benjamin
Powell. Annual index. Cumulative index,
1934-61. Indexed in Writings on American
History, 1934-; America: History and Life,
1963-.

Pennsylvania Magazine of History and Biography
                              1877-   Q $10
      Hist. Soc. of Pennsylvania, 1300 Locust
St., Philadelphia, 19109. Annual index.
Cumulative index, 1877-1951. Indexed in
Writings on American History, 1902-; Histor-
ical Abstracts, 1955-63; America: History
and Life, 1964-.

Picket Post; A Record of Patriotism
                                               $3
      Valley Forge Hist. Soc., Valley Forge,
19481. Indexed in Writings on American History, 1948-.

Radnor Historical Society Bulletin
                              5/yr. $3
      W. Beech Tree Lane, Wayne, 19087. Ed.
William Fletcher. Index in preparation.

Settler
                              1938-   Q $3
      Bradford Co. Hist. Soc., Towanda, 18848.
  Cumulative index, 1938-73.

Stepping Stones
                              1955-   3/yr. $2
      Warren Co. Hist. Soc., Box 427, Warren,
  16365. Ed. Dr. Ernest C. Miller. Cumulative
  index, 1955-70.

Town Crier
                              1965-   Q $3
      Quakertown Hist. Soc., 44 S. Main St.,
  Quakertown, 18961. Ed. Lillian Shaw. Not
  indexed.

Trolley Fare
                              1955-   M $6
      Pennsylvania Railway Mus. Assoc., Inc.,
  Box 832, Pittsburgh, 15230. Ed. Harold England. Not indexed.

Venango Intelligencer
                                               $3
      Venango Co. Hist. Soc., Box 101, Frank-
  lin, 16323. Ed. William K. Bowen.

Western Pennsylvania Historical Magazine
                              1918-   Q $10
      Hist. Soc. of Western Pennsylvania,
  4338 Bigelow Blvd., Pittsburgh, 15213.
  Annual index. Cumulative index, v. 1-43/
  1918-60. Indexed in Writings on American
  History, 1918-; America: History and Life,
  1965-.

RHODE ISLAND

The Flyer
>   1970-   M $10
>   Old Slater Mill Mus., Box 727, Paw-
> tucket, 02862. Ed. Patrick Malone. Not in-
> dexed.

Hinterland
>   Western Rhode Island Civic Hist. Soc.,
> Providence, 02909.

The Newport Gazette
>   1947-   Q $15
>   Preservation Soc. of Newport Co., Wash-
> ington Sq., Newport, 02840. Ed. Mrs. L. J.
> Panaggio. Not indexed.

Newport History
>   1900- $10
>   Formerly Newport Historical Society
> Bulletin. 82 Touro St., Newport, 02840. Ed.
> Mrs. Edward G. Crosly. Cumulative indexes,
> 1900-71. Indexed in Writings on American
> History, 1912-.

Pettaquamscutt Reporter
>   1958-   5/yr. $5
>   Pettaquamscutt Hist. Soc., 1348 Kings-
> town Rd., Kingston, 02881. Eds. Clarince
> and William Metz. Cumulative index on cards.

Rhode Island History
>   1942-   Q $15
>   Formerly Rhode Island Historical Society
> Collections, 1827-1941. 52 Power St., Provi-
> dence, 02906. Ed. Nancy F. Chudocoff. Index
> at society office. Indexed in Writings on
> American History, 1902-; Abstracts of Folk-
> lore Studies, 1972; America: History and
> Life, 1963-.

Rhode Island Jewish Historical Notes
                          1954-   A $12
        130 Sessions St., Providence, 02906.
    Ed. Seebert J. Goldowsky. Annual index.

                    SOUTH CAROLINA

Drover's Post
                          1969-   S-A $5
        Spartanburg Co. Hist. Assoc., Box 245,
    Spartanburg, 29302. Eds. Mrs. W. C. Herbert
    and Mrs. Webb Thomson.

Independent Republic Quarterly
                          1967-   Q $5
        Horry Co. Hist. Soc., Conway, 29526.
    Not indexed.

Mortar and Pestle
                          1970-   Q $5
        Georgetown Co. Hist. Comm., Box 902,
    Georgetown, 29440. Ed. Dennis T. Lawson.
    Not indexed.

New South Carolina State Gazette
        South Carolina Dept. of Archives and
    Hist., 1430 Senate St., Columbia, 29211.

Newberry Historical Society Bulletin
                          1970-   S-A $3
        Box 364, Newberry, 29108. Ed. M. Foster
    Farley. Not indexed.

Orangeburg Historical and Genealogical Society
Record   1969-   Q $5
        Box 1616, College Sta., Orangeburg,
    29115. Not indexed.

Preservation Progress
                                    1953-   Q $10
        Preservation Soc. of Charleston, Box
521, Charleston, 29401.   Ed. Robert Stockton.
Not indexed.

South Carolina Historical Magazine
                                    1900-   Q $15
        Formerly South Carolina Historical and
Genealogical Magazine.   South Carolina Hist.
Soc., 100 Meeting St., Fireproof Bldg.,
Charleston, 29401.   Ed. Miss Elise Pinckney.
Consolidated index, v. 1-40/1900-39, with
subject index, v. 1-61/1900-60.   Indexed in
Writings on American History, 1902-; Amer-
ica: History and Life, 1963-; Abstracts of
English Studies, 1965, 1969.

South Carolina History Illustrated
                                    1970-73 Q
        Indexed.

                    SOUTH DAKOTA

James Valley Historical Society Quarterly
                                    1973-   Q $15
        Box 397, Huron, 57350.   Eds. Louella
Barrows and Dorothy Grover.   Not indexed.

The Sabers
        Old Ft. Meade Mus. and Hist. Research
Assoc., Box 432, Sturgis, 57785.

South Dakota Historical Review
                                    1935-37
        South Dakota Hist. Soc.   Indexed in
Writings on American History, 1935-37.

South Dakota History
                              1970-   Q $5
     South Dakota State Hist. Soc., Soldiers
and Sailors Memorial Bldg., Pierre, 57501.
Ed. Ms. Jan Dykshorn. Index to each v.
printed in first issue of succeeding v.

South Dakota Report and Historical Collections
                      1902-   B-E
     Formerly South Dakota Historical Col-
lections, v. 1-23; South Dakota Historical
Collections and Report, v. 24-27. Printed
index, v. 1-16. Indexed in Writings on
American History, 1934-36.

Wi-iyohi
                            1947-70 M
     Printed index, v. 1-20 in v. 21. Not
indexed, 1968-70. Indexed in Writings on
American History, 1950-.

                    TENNESSEE

Annals of Lawrence Co.
                         1970-   Q
     Lawrence Co. Hist. Soc., Box 431,
Lawrenceburg, 38464. Annual index.

Chattanews
     Chattanooga Area Hist. Assoc., Box
1663, Chattanooga, 37401.

Coffee County Historical Society Quarterly
                         1970-   Q $7.50
     Box 524, Chester, 37355. Ed. Betty Ann
Bridgewater. Not indexed.

Courier
                       1964-   3/yr. Free
     Tennessee Hist. Comm., 403 7th Ave., N.,
Nashville, 37219. Ed. Ilene J. Cornwell.
Not indexed.

Discipliana
                          1941-   Q
        Formerly Harbinger and Discipliana.
    Disciples of Christ Hist. Soc., 1101 19th
    Ave. S., Nashville, 37212. Cumulative index,
    1941-66.

East Tennessee Historical Society Publications
                          1929-   A
        McGhee Library, Knoxville, 37902.
    Cumulative index, v. 1-20, 21-35. Indexed in
    Writings on American History, 1929-.

Echoes
                          1955-   Q $5
        East Tennessee Hist. Soc., McGhee Li-
    brary, Knoxville, 37902. Cumulative index,
    v. 1-5.

Frow Chips
                          1971-   M $5
        Rutherford Co. Hist. Soc., Box 1139,
    Murfreesboro, 37130. Ed. Homer Pittard. Not
    indexed.

Historic Maury
                          1965-   Q $4
        Maury Co. Hist. Soc, 210 1st Ave.,
    Mt. Pleasant, 38474. Annual index. Cumu-
    lative index, v. 1-3.

Historic Nashville Quarterly
                          1975-   Q $25
        Box 40342, 37204. Not indexed.

Historical Society of Roane County
                          1970-   10/yr.
        Formerly Roane County Historical Society
    Newsletter. Rockwood, 37854. Not indexed.

Lincoln County Tennessee Pioneers
                          1970-   Q
        Lincoln Co. Hist. Soc., Inc., 202 E.
    Washington, Fayetteville, 37334. Annual
    index.

M V C Bulletin
                              1947-   A $5
        West Tennessee Hist. Soc., Mississippi
Valley Collection, Brister Library, Memphis
State Univ., 38111. Annual index. Cumu-
lative index.

Marshall County Historical Quarterly
                              1970-   Q
        Annual index.

Montgomery County Genealogical Journal
                              1971-   Q $3
        Montgomery Co. Hist. Soc., 512 Madison
St., Clarksville, 37040. Annual index.

Rutherford County Historical Society Publication   1973-   S-A
        Box 1139, Murfreesboro, 37130. Not in-
dexed.

Studies in Polk County History
                              1965-?
        Polk Co. Hist. Soc., Benton, 37307.

Tennessee Historical Quarterly
                              1942-   Q $5
        Formerly Tennessee Historical Magazine.
Tennessee Hist. Soc., Nashville, 37219.
Annual index. Cumulative index, 1942-1966.
Indexed in Writings on American History,
1948-; Historical Abstracts, 1963; America:
History and Life, 1964-.

West Tennessee Historical Society Papers
                              1947-   A
        Brister Library, Memphis State Univ.,
Memphis, 38111. Cumulative index, v. 1-10,
11-20.

Williamson County Historical Society JOurnal
                              1970-   A
        Annual index.

TEXAS

El Campanario
                          1970-   Q $10
     Texas Old Missions and Fts. Restoration
Assoc., 524 N. 22nd St., Waco, 76707.   Ed.
Henrietta Henry.

Chronicles of Smith County
                          1962-   S-A $5
     Formerly Chronicles.   Smith Co. Hist.
Soc. and Survey Committee, Rt. 6, Box 310-C,
Tyler, 75701.   Ed. Lucille Mardock.   Cumu-
lative index, v. 1-10.

East Texas Historical Journal
                          1963-   S-A
     East Texas Hist. Assoc., Box 6223, Nacog-
doches, 75961.   Indexed in Texas, 1970-.

Edwards Plateau Historian
                          1965-   Irreg. $5
     Edwards Plateau Hist. Assoc., Water
Valley, 76958.   Ed. Elton Mims.   Cumulative
index, 1967-68.

Harrison County Historical Herald
                          1964-   Irreg.
     Harrison Co. Hist. Soc., Peter Whetstone
Sq., Marshall, 75670.   "An index is kept with
the file."   Not published, 1971-73.

Heritage Highlights
     Cooke Co. Heritage Soc., Inc., Box 150,
Gainesville, 76240.

Local History and Genealogical Society Quarterly
                          1955-   Q $7.50
     Hacienda Tejas, 2515 Sweetbrier Dr.,
Dallas, 75228.   Ed. Minnie Champ.   Annual index.

News from the Frontier Fort on the Conchos
                        1969-   Q   Free
     Cover title: Fort Concho Report.   Ft.
Concho Restoration and Mus., 716 Burges St.,
San Angelo, 76901.   Ed. Carol Schmidt.   Not
indexed.

Panhandle-Plains Historical Review
                        1928-   A
     Panhandle-Plains Hist. Soc., 2400 4th
Ave., Canyon, 79016.   Annual index.   Cumulative index, 1928-72.

Password
                        1956-   Q $10
     El Paso Co. Hist. Soc., Civic Center
Plaza, 79901.   Ed. Conrey Bryson.   Annual
index.   Cumulative index, 1956-70.   Indexed
in Writings on American History, 1960.

Southwestern Historical Quarterly
                        1897-   Q $10
     Formerly Quarterly of the Texas State
Historical Association.   306 University Sta.,
Austin, 78712.   Ed. J. B. Frantz.   Annual
index.   Cumulative index.   Indexed in Writ-
ings on American History, 1902-; Historical
Abstracts, 1955-63; America: History and
Life, 1964-; Social Science Citation Index.

Texana
                                  Q $7.50
     Box 1984, Waco, 76703.   Ed. Robert E.
Davis.   Indexed in America: History and Life,
1964-; Texas, 1970-.

Texas Historian
                        1941-   5/yr. $3
     Formerly Junior Historian.   Texas State
Hist. Assoc., Richardson Hall, Univ. Sta.,
Austin, 78712.   Ed. J. B. Frantz.   Indexed
in Writings on American History, 1948-;
Texas, 1970-; Subject Index to Children's
Magazines.

Valor
                    1971-   S-A $8
        Hood's Texas Brigade Assoc., Hill Jr.
    College, Hillsboro, 76645.   Ed. H. B. Simpson.
    Not indexed.

Waco Heritage and History
        Historic Waco Found., Inc.

                    UTAH

Our Pioneer Heritage
                         A $5
        Daughters of Utah Pioneers, 300 N.
    Main St., Salt Lake City, 84103.   Ed. Kate
    B. Carter.   Annual index.   Cumulative index
    on cards.

The Pioneer
                    1936-   B-M $7
        National Soc. of the Sons of Utah
    Pioneers, 2998 Connor St., Salt Lake, 84109.
    Ed. Marvin E. Smith.

Utah Genealogical and Historical Magazine
                    1910-40
        Genealogical Soc. of Utah.   Indexed in
    Writings on American History, 1910-40.

Utah Historical Quarterly
                    1928-   Q $7
        Utah State Hist. Soc., 603 E. South
    Temple, Salt Lake, 84102.   Annual index.
    Working on complete cumulative index based
    on card file kept at society.   Indexed in
    Writings on American History, 1931-; America:
    History and Life, 1963-; Peace Research Ab-
    stracts Journal.

VERMONT

Chittenden County Historical Society Bulletin
                          1965-   Irreg. $3
      Bailey Library, University of Vermont,
   Burlington, 05401. Ed. Lincoln C. Brownall.

Chittenden County Historical Society Heritage
Series Pamphlet   1972-   Irreg. $3 ea.
      Bailey Library, University of Vermont,
   Burlington, 05401. Ed. Lilian B. Carlisle.

Rokeby Messenger
                          1960-   Irreg.
      Rowland E. Robinson Memorial Assoc.,
   Ferrisburg, 05456. Not indexed.

Rutland Historical Society Quarterly
                          1970-   Q $2
      101 Center St., Rutland, 05701. Not
   indexed.

Vermont Historical Society Proceedings
                          1860-26/28, 1929-43
      Cumulative index, 1860-1910, 1930-42.
   Proceedings are analyzed in the card catalog,
   Bailey Library, University of Vermont. Bur-
   lington, 05401.

Vermont History
                          1954-   Q $7.50
      Vermont Hist. Soc., Pavilion Bldg.,
   Montpelier, 05602. Annual index. Indexed in
   Writings on American History, 1954-; America:
   History and Life, 1963-.

Vermont Life
                          1946-   Q $3.50
      61 Elm St., Montpelier, 05602. Cumulative
   index, 1946-66. Indexed in Writings on American History, 1949-; Abstracts of Folklore
   Studies, 1967-.

Vermont Old Cemetery Association Bulletin
                         1961-   Irreg.
      308 S. Prospect St., Burlington, 05401.
   Not indexed.

Vermont Quarterly
                    1943-53 Q
      Cumulative index, 1943-52. Indexed in
   Writings on American History, 1948-53.

Vermonter
                    1895-1945
      Cumulative index, 1914-39. Card index
   for 1940-45 housed in Bailey Library, University of Vermont, Burlington, 05401.

                    VIRGINIA

Archeological Society of Virginia Quarterly
Bulletin   1946-   Q $4
      1946 Lansing Ave., Richmond, 23225.
   Indexed through v. 25.

Arlington Historical Magazine
                    1957-   A $5
      Box 402, Arlington, 22210. Ed. Sandra J.
   Boyle. Annual index. Indexed in Writings on
   American History, 1958-.

Augusta Historical Bulletin
                    1965-   S-A $10
      Augusta Co. Hist. Soc., Box 686,
   Staunton, 24401. Cumulative index printed
   every 5 years.

Goochland County Historical Society Magazine
            River Rd., Rt. 6, Goochland, 23063.

King and Queen County Historical Society Bulletin   1956-   2/yr $2
        King and Queen, 23085. Ed. Mrs. Irman
Johnson. Not indexed.

Loudoun County Historical Society Bulletin
        Box 344, Leesburg, 22075.

Magazine of Albermarle County History
                                1940-   A $5
        The Library, Univ. of Virginia, Charlot-
tsville, 22903. Ed. Michall Plunkett. Cumulative index, v. 1-19. Cumulative index on
cards for v. 20-30.

Northern Neck of Virginia Historical Magazine
                                1951-   A $7.50
        Box 156, Montross, 22520. Ed. Charles
W. H. Warner. Cumulative index in progress.
Indexed in Writings on American History,
1951-.

Roanoke Historical Society Journal
                                1964-   S-A $1.50
        Box 1904, Roanoke, 24008.

V H M F Newsletter
                                1976-   Q $10
        Newport News, 23604. Not indexed.

Virginia Baptist Register
                                1962-   A $2.50
        Box 95, Univ. of Richmond, 23173. Cum-
ulative index, 1962-66, 1967-71.

Virginia Cavalcade
                                1951-   Q $3
        Virginia State Library, Richmond, 23219.
Analytic cards are published for each article
and sold in sets to libraries. Indexed in
Writings on American History, 1951-; America:
History and Life, 1963-.

Virginia Historic Landmarks Commission Notes on
Virginia   1971-   Q
        1116 9th St., State Office Bldg., Rich-
mond, 23219. Not indexed.

Virginia Magazine of History and Biography
                            1893-   Q $8
        Virginia Hist. Soc., Box 7311, Richmond,
23221. Annual index. Indexed up to 1930 in
Earl G. Swen's Virginia Historical Index.
Virginia State Hist. Soc. has made analytic
cards since 1930. Indexed in Writings on
American History, 1906-; Historical Abstracts
1955-63; America: History and Life, 1964-.

Virginia Phoenix
                            1968-   S-A
        Virginia Hist. Federation, 12th and
Capitol Sts., Richmond, 23219. Not indexed.

Wythe County Historical Review
                            1971-   S-A $5
        Wytheville, 24382. Ed. Helen H. Grove.
Not indexed.

                    WASHINGTON

Cowlitz County Historical Quarterly
                                         $3
        4th and Church Sts., Kelso, 98626. Ed.
Mary Clanfield.

Franklin Flyer
                            1968-   Q $3
        Franklin Co. Hist. Soc., Box 1033, Paso,
99301. Ed. Walter A. Oberst. Cumulative index, v. 1-4.

Lake Chelan History Notes
        Lake Chelan Hist. Soc., Box 697, Chelan,
98816.

Okanogan County Heritage

                    1963-   Q $8
    Okanogan Co. Hist. Soc., Box 1129, Okan-
ogan, 98840.   Eds. Charles and Mary Kerr.
Cumulative index, v. 1-10.

Pacific Northwest Quarterly

                    1906-   Q $5
    Formerly Washington Historical Quarter-
ly.   Washington State Hist. Soc., 315 N.
Stadium Way, Tacoma, 98403.   Indexed in
Writings on American History, 1912-; Historical Abstracts, 1955-63; America: History and
Life, 1964-; Abstracts of Folklore Studies,
1967-.

Pacific Northwesterner

                    1956-   Q $3
    Spokane Corral of the Westerners, Box
1717, Spokane, 99210.   Indexed in Writings on
American History, 1957, 1960-.

Past Time

                    1968-   Irreg. $15
    Seattle Hist. Soc., 2161 E. Hamlin St.,
Seattle, 98112.   ed. Mary Anne Fleck.   Not
indexed.

Sea Chest

                    1967-   Q $10
    Puget Sound Maritime Hist. Soc., Inc.,
2161 E. Hamlin St., Seattle, 98112.   Ed. Hal
H. Will.   Annual index.   Cumulative index.

Skamania County Heritage

                    1972-   Q $2
    Skamania Co. Hist. Mus., Vancouver Ave.,
Stevenson, 98648.   Ed. Ruth Hill Strong.   Index on cards.

Sounder

                    1957-   M $20
    Pudget Sound Railway Hist. Soc., Box
3801, Seattle, 98124.   Ed. Judy Bunting.   Not
indexed.

Sou'wester
                              1966-   M $3
        Pacific Co. Hist. Soc. and Mus. Found.,
Inc., Box 384, Raymond, 98577. Annual index.
Cumulative index, 1966-73.

WEST VIRGINIA

Greenbrier Historical Society Journal
                              1963-   A $4
        Lewisburg, 24901. Ed. Kenneth D. Swope.
Not indexed.

Harrison County Historical Society Newsletter
                              1972-   B-A $5
        123 W. Main St., Clarksburg, 26301. Ed.
Mrs. Bond Davis. Not indexed.

Mineral County Historical Society Bulletin
                              1972-   Q
        35 E. Queen St., Keyer, 26726.

Randolph County Historical Society Magazine of
History and Biography   1924-   Irreg. $2
        Box 1164, Elkins, 26241. Not indexed.

West Virginia History
                              1939-   Q $5
        State Dept. of Archives and Hist., State
Capitol Bldg., Charleston, 25305. Annual
index. Indexed in Writings on American History, 1939-; America: History and Life, 1966-.

WISCONSIN

Anchor News
>   1969-   M $4
>   Formerly Redfin News.   Manitowoc Submarine Memorial Assoc., Inc., 402 N. 8th St. Manitowoc, 54220.   Not indexed.

Badger History
>   1947-   9/yr. $4
>   State Hist. Soc. of Wisconsin, 816 State St., Madison, 53706.   Indexed in Subject Index to Children's Magazines.

Badger Postal History
>   1961-   Q
>   Wisconsin Postal Hist. Soc.

Brown Deer Historical Society, Inc. Newsletter
>   1961-   Q
>   Brown Deer, 53223.

Exchange, A Newsletter for County and Local Historical Societies and Museums
>   1958-   3/yr.
>   State Hist. Soc. of Wisconsin, 816 State St., Madison, 53706.

Flashbacks
>   1962(?)- 3/yr.
>   United Methodist Hist. Soc., Sun Prairie, 53590.

Gazette
>   1962-   M
>   Formerly Mid-Continent Railway Gazette; The Railway Gazette.   Mid-Continent Railway Hist. Soc., North Freedom, 53951.

The Historical Messenger
                              1941-   Q $7.50
       Milwaukee Co. Hist. Soc., 910 N., 3rd.
   St., Milwaukee, 53203.   Cumulative index,
   1941-62; 1963-67.

Inscriptions
                              1972-   5/yr.
       Wisconsin State Old Cemetery Soc.,
   4319 N. 70th St., Milwaukee, 53216.

Landmark
                              1958-   Q $3
       Waukesha Co. Hist. Soc., 20245 W.
   National Ave., New Berlin, 53151.   Annual
   index.   Cumulative index, 1958-.

Lore
                                                 $12.50
       Milwaukee Public Mus., c/o Robert Gor-
   ski, 800 N. Wells St., Milwaukee.

Manitowoc County Historical Society Newsletter
                              1966-   5/yr. $3
       1115 N. 18th St., Manitowoc, 54220.
   Ed. Edward Ehlert.

Milwaukee County Historical Society Newsletter
                              1951-   M
       910 N. 3rd St., Milwaukee, 53203.

Museum Memo
                              1973-   Q
       State Hist. Soc. of Wisconsin, 816 State
   St., Madison, 53706.

Pinery
                              1956-   Irreg.
       Portage Co. Hist. Soc., 301 Post Rd.,
   Stevens Point, 54467.   Typed cumulative index, 1956-.

Pioneer Village Review
                              1971-   Q
        Ozaukee Co. Hist. Soc., 533 N. Meguon
St., Cedarburg, 53012.

Rock County Recorder
                              1971-   Irreg. $5
        Rock Co. Hist. Soc., 440 N. Jackson St.
Janesville, 53545.   Ed. Judith Hamilton.
Not indexed.

Shortcircuit
                              1974-   A
        Wisconsin Electric Railway Hist. Soc.,
Inc., 2002 Church St., East Troy, 53120.

Soundings
                              1959-   Q? $8
        Wisconsin Marine Historical Soc., 814
W. Wisconsin Ave., Milwaukee, 53233.   Ed.
Orval Liljequist.

Southport Newsletter
                              1933?-   B-M $3
        Formerly Kenosha County Historical Soc-
iety Bulletin.   6300 3rd. Ave., Kenosha,
53140.

Staff
                              1962?-   Irreg.
        State Hist. Soc. of Wisconsin, 816
State St., Madison, 53706.

Waukesha County Historical Society Newsletter
                              1972-   Q
        101 W. Main St., Waukesha, 53186.

Wisconsin Electric Lines
                              1968?-   Q $7.50
        Wisconsin Electric Railway Hist. Soc.,
Inc., Box 726, East Troy, 53120.   Ed. William
F. Midden.

Wisconsin Ledger
                         1972-   Q   Free
      Wisconsin American Revolution Bicen-
tennial Comm., 816 State St., Madison, 53706.

Wisconsin Magazine of History
                         1917-   Q $10
      State Hist. Soc. of Wisconsin, 816 State
St., Madison, 53706. Ed. Paul Hass. Annual
index. Cumulative index every 10 yrs. Indexed in Writings on American History, 1917-;
America: History and Life, 1964-; Abstracts
of Folklore Studies, 1969, 1972.

Wisconsin State Historical Society Bulletin
                         1894-
      816 State St., Madison, 53706. Publi-
cation suspended 1933-55. No. 100, 1956
called new series.

Wisconsin State Historical Society Collections
                         1854-1931
      Publication suspended 1859-67. Cumu-
lative index, v. 1-20/1854-1911 in v. 21.
Indexed in Writings on American History, 1903-
18.

Wisconsin State Historical Society Proceedings
                         1874-
      Formerly its Collections. Cumulative
index, 1874-1901. Indexed in Writings on
American History, 1902-32.

Wisconsin State Historical Society Publications
      Indexed in Writings on American History,
1926-40.

Wisconsin Then and Now
                         1954-   M
      State Hist. Soc. of Wisconsin, 816 State
St., Madison, 53706. Ed. Marilyn Dilley.
Included with a subscription to the Wisconsin
Magazine of History. Indexed in America:
History and Life, 1963-; Abstracts of Folk-
lore Studies, 1970.

WYOMING

Annals of Wyoming
                    1923-   S-A $5
     Formerly Quarterly Bulletin. Wyoming
State Archives and Hist. Dept., State Office
Bldg., Cheyenne, 82001. Ed. Katherine
Halverson. Annual index, 1943-69. Cumu-
lative index, 1923-42, 1943-59. Indexed in
Writings on American History, 1925-; Amer-
ica: History and Life, 1963-.

Wyoming History News
                    1953-   B-M
     Formerly History News. Wyoming State
Archives and Hist. Dept., State Office Bldg.,
Cheyenne, 82001. Ed. Katherine Halverson.
Included with subscription to Annals of
Wyoming. Not indexed.

TITLE INDEX

H

I

J   cop.1

M

N

O

P

S

T

122

124

Y